LLM Graph RAG

A Hands-on Guide to Building Advanced, Graph-Based Retrieval-
Augmented Generation with LLMs

©

Written By

Maxime Lane

Copyright

LLM Graph RAG: A Hands-on Guide to Building Advanced, Graph-Based Retrieval-Augmented Generation with LLMs

Author: Maxime Lane

Table of Content

Preface

Welcome to **LLM Graph RAG: A Hands-on Guide to Building Advanced, Graph-Based Retrieval-Augmented Generation with LLMs**. This book is designed to be a comprehensive resource for anyone interested in exploring and building advanced AI systems that combine the power of large language models (LLMs) with graph-based retrieval-augmented generation (RAG). In this preface, we outline the purpose of the book, acknowledge those who contributed, introduce the authors, and provide guidance on how to get the most out of this text. We also explain the conventions and notations used throughout the book.

Acknowledgments

We would like to extend our heartfelt thanks to everyone who contributed to the development of this book. Special acknowledgments are due to:

- **Colleagues and Peers:**
  For their invaluable feedback and critical insights, which have greatly improved the quality of the content.
- **Research Collaborators:**
  Whose pioneering work in the fields of language models, graph theory, and information retrieval has laid the foundation for this guide.
- **Industry Professionals and Educators:**
  For sharing real-world challenges and use cases that helped shape the practical sections of this book.
- **Family and Friends:**
  For their unwavering support and encouragement during the long hours of research and writing.

Each contribution has helped transform this guide into a resource that we believe will be both educational and inspirational for its readers.

Who Should Read This Book

This guide is intended for a wide range of readers, including:

- **AI Practitioners and Developers:**
  Who are looking to implement and optimize advanced retrieval-augmented generation systems using LLMs and graph-based techniques.
- **Researchers and Academics:**
  Interested in the latest methodologies and practical applications in the intersection of language models, graph theory, and information retrieval.
- **Students and Enthusiasts:**
  Who have a basic understanding of machine learning and are eager to explore new paradigms in AI development.
- **Industry Professionals:**
  Seeking to enhance their technical knowledge with cutting-edge techniques that can be applied to real-world problems, such as data management, customer support, or information retrieval systems.

No matter your background, if you are eager to learn about building systems that combine robust language understanding with innovative graph-based data retrieval, this book is designed for you.

How to Use This Book

This book is structured to guide you through both the theoretical foundations and practical applications of LLM Graph RAG systems. Here are some suggestions on how to make the best use of this guide:

1. **Read Sequentially:**
   The book is organized in a logical progression from introductory concepts to advanced implementations. We recommend reading the chapters in order, especially if you are new to any of the topics covered.
2. **Hands-On Practice:**
   Throughout the book, you will find code examples, tables, and step-by-step tutorials. It is highly recommended that you follow along

using the provided code snippets and complete the exercises to reinforce your understanding.

3. **Reference as Needed:**
   If you are already familiar with some of the concepts, feel free to jump to the sections that are most relevant to your current needs. Each chapter is designed to be somewhat self-contained, so you can refer back to specific sections as a resource.

4. **Use Supplementary Materials:**
   In addition to the printed text, code repositories and supplementary resources are available online. These resources include updated code examples, additional readings, and a community forum where you can ask questions and share insights.

5. **Keep a Notebook:**
   Consider maintaining a learning journal where you can jot down key concepts, code notes, and questions as you progress through the chapters. This can be an invaluable resource as you apply the techniques in your projects.

Conventions and Notations

To maintain clarity and consistency throughout this book, we have adopted several conventions and notations. Below is an overview of the key formatting and terminology guidelines:

General Conventions

- **Headings and Subheadings:**
  Chapters, sections, and subsections are clearly labeled with numbered headings (e.g., 1.1, 2.3.1) to help you easily navigate the content.
- **Code Examples:**
  All code examples are provided in Python. Each example is explained in detail, with comments to help you understand the purpose and function of each code block.
- **Tables and Figures:**
  Important information is summarized in tables and illustrated with diagrams where appropriate. Each table and figure includes a caption that explains its context and relevance.

Notations and Terminology

Symbol/Term	Meaning/Usage
LLM	Large Language Model – A model that is pre-trained on a vast corpus of text data.
RAG	Retrieval-Augmented Generation – A technique that combines retrieval of external information with text generation.
GNN	Graph Neural Network – A neural network architecture designed to work with graph-structured data.
API	Application Programming Interface – A set of rules that allows programs to interact with each other.

- **Mathematical Notations:**
  Where mathematical equations are necessary, we will use standard symbols and ensure that each variable is clearly defined in the accompanying text.
- **Terminology:**
  Specialized terms will be defined when first introduced. A glossary is provided in Appendix A for quick reference to key terms.

By following these conventions, we aim to ensure that the material is accessible, easy to follow, and unambiguous, regardless of your prior experience with the topics covered.

Chapter 1: Introduction to LLM Graph RAG

Graph-based Retrieval-Augmented Generation (RAG) systems represent a cutting-edge approach to improving the capabilities of large language models (LLMs) by integrating structured knowledge retrieval from graph databases. This chapter lays the foundation for understanding how LLMs have evolved, the role of RAG systems in AI, and the benefits and challenges associated with this approach.

1.1 The Evolution of Language Models

1.1.1 From Rule-Based Systems to Deep Learning

Before deep learning revolutionized natural language processing (NLP), most language models were built using rule-based and statistical approaches. These early systems had significant limitations in understanding context, handling variability in language, and scaling efficiently.

Rule-Based Language Processing

In the early days of AI, computers processed language using explicit rules written by linguists and programmers. These rules attempted to define the structure and meaning of language using syntax trees, dictionaries, and manually crafted patterns.

Example of a Simple Rule-Based NLP System:

```python
def simple_response(user_input):
    """A basic rule-based chatbot that responds to greetings."""
    responses = {
        "hello": "Hi there! How can I help you?",
        "how are you": "I'm a program, so I don't have feelings, but I'm here to assist you!",
        "goodbye": "Goodbye! Have a great day!"
    }
```

```
    user_input = user_input.lower()
    return responses.get(user_input, "I'm sorry, I don't
understand that.")

# Example usage
print(simple_response("hello"))
print(simple_response("how are you"))
```

Limitations of Rule-Based Systems:

- Rigid and difficult to scale.
- Unable to handle unseen variations in user input.
- Poor generalization beyond predefined rules.

Statistical Language Models

The next major advancement was statistical methods, which involved analyzing large text corpora to derive probabilities of word occurrences.

For example, **n-gram models** estimate the probability of a word based on the previous n-1 words:

$$P(wn|wn-1,wn-2,...,w1)$$

While these models improved performance, they still lacked deep contextual understanding.

Neural Networks and Deep Learning

With the rise of deep learning, researchers began using neural networks for NLP tasks. Early architectures like Recurrent Neural Networks (RNNs) allowed models to process sequences of text, but they struggled with long-term dependencies.

A major breakthrough came with the introduction of **Transformers** (Vaswani et al., 2017), which enabled models to understand text at scale by using self-attention mechanisms.

Table 1.1: Evolution of Language Models

Era	Model Type	Key Features	Limitations
1950s-1980s	Rule-Based Systems	Predefined rules for language	Rigid, cannot generalize well
1990s-2000s	Statistical Models	Probability-based language modeling	Limited context understanding
2010s	Deep Learning (RNNs)	Sequential learning of text data	Struggles with long-range dependencies
2017-Present	Transformers (LLMs)	Self-attention for long-context modeling	Requires large-scale training data

1.1.2 The Rise of Large Language Models

Large Language Models (LLMs) like GPT-3, GPT-4, and BERT have demonstrated an unprecedented ability to process and generate human-like text. These models are pre-trained on massive datasets using deep learning techniques and can perform a wide range of NLP tasks, including text generation, translation, and summarization.

How LLMs Work

LLMs are based on the **Transformer architecture**, which consists of:

1. **Self-Attention Mechanisms** – Allow models to consider all words in a sentence at once, rather than processing them sequentially.
2. **Positional Encoding** – Enables the model to retain word order.
3. **Pre-training and Fine-tuning** – LLMs are first trained on vast datasets and later fine-tuned for specific tasks.

Example: Text Generation with GPT

Using OpenAI's GPT API, we can generate text dynamically:

```python
import openai

def generate_text(prompt):
```

```
    """Generate a response using an LLM API (GPT-like
model)."""
    response = openai.ChatCompletion.create(
        model="gpt-4",
        messages=[{"role": "user", "content": prompt}]
    )
    return response["choices"][0]["message"]["content"]

# Example usage
print(generate_text("What is the role of transformers in
NLP?"))
```

This example demonstrates how LLMs use pre-trained knowledge to generate human-like text.

Advantages of LLMs

- **High Fluency:** Generates text that is coherent and contextually relevant.
- **Adaptability:** Can be fine-tuned for specific domains.
- **Scalability:** Can process large-scale datasets efficiently.

Challenges of LLMs

- **Memory Constraints:** Large-scale training requires significant computational power.
- **Hallucination Issues:** Models may generate factually incorrect or misleading text.
- **Lack of Explainability:** Understanding how the model arrives at an answer is difficult.

1.2 Overview of Retrieval-Augmented Generation (RAG)

1.2.1 Definition and Historical Context

Retrieval-Augmented Generation (RAG) is a hybrid approach that combines:

- **Retrieval Models** – Fetch relevant external data.
- **Generative Models** – Use the retrieved data to generate a more accurate response.

Instead of relying solely on internalized knowledge (as LLMs do), RAG dynamically **retrieves** information from a **document store**, knowledge graph, or external database before generating text.

How RAG Works

1. **User Query:** The user asks a question.
2. **Retrieval Component:** The system searches a knowledge base for relevant documents.
3. **Augmentation Step:** The retrieved documents are fed into an LLM.
4. **Generation Component:** The LLM synthesizes an answer based on both the query and the retrieved documents.

Example: A Simple RAG System

```python
from transformers import RagTokenizer, RagRetriever,
RagSequenceForGeneration

# Load pre-trained RAG model
tokenizer = RagTokenizer.from_pretrained("facebook/rag-token-base")
retriever = RagRetriever.from_pretrained("facebook/rag-token-base")
model =
RagSequenceForGeneration.from_pretrained("facebook/rag-token-base")

def generate_rag_response(query):
    """Generate a response using a RAG model."""
    inputs = tokenizer(query, return_tensors="pt")
    retrieved_docs = retriever.retrieve(query,
inputs["input_ids"])
    response = model.generate(input_ids=inputs["input_ids"])
    return tokenizer.decode(response[0],
skip_special_tokens=True)

# Example usage
print(generate_rag_response("What is retrieval-augmented
generation?"))
```

1.2.2 Benefits and Challenges

Benefits of RAG

1. **Improved Accuracy:** By incorporating external knowledge, RAG reduces factual errors.
2. **Scalability:** Can adapt to various domains by retrieving domain-specific knowledge.
3. **Up-to-Date Information:** Can retrieve real-time data instead of relying on outdated pre-trained knowledge.

Challenges of RAG

1. **Retrieval Latency:** Searching a database can slow down response times.
2. **Data Quality Issues:** The accuracy of RAG depends on the quality of retrieved documents.
3. **Integration Complexity:** Combining retrieval and generation requires sophisticated system design.

1.3 The Role of Graph-Based Methods

Graph-based methods are essential for structuring and organizing information in a way that enhances retrieval and reasoning capabilities. These methods are particularly useful in **retrieval-augmented generation (RAG) systems**, where the ability to find relevant information efficiently is crucial.

1.3.1 Introduction to Graph Theory

What is Graph Theory?

Graph theory is a field of mathematics that studies relationships between entities. In computer science and artificial intelligence, graphs are widely used to represent **networks, relationships, and structured knowledge**.

A **graph** consists of:

- **Nodes (or vertices):** Represent entities such as documents, words, people, or concepts.
- **Edges:** Represent relationships between nodes (e.g., "is related to," "works for," "cited by").

Basic Components of Graphs

Term	Definition	Example
Node (Vertex)	A single entity in the graph	A person in a social network
Edge	A connection between two nodes	A friendship between two people
Weighted Edge	An edge with a numerical value representing strength or importance	The similarity between two documents
Directed Graph	A graph where edges have a direction (A → B)	Citation network (one paper cites another)
Undirected Graph	A graph where edges have no direction (A ↔ B)	Social network (mutual friendship)

Example: Representing a Simple Graph

Consider a graph where **three researchers** collaborate on AI projects.

```pgsql
      Alice
      /     \
  (Works with)
    /           \
  Bob ------->  Charlie
   (Collaborates on AI)
```

This structure can be represented programmatically in Python:

```python
import networkx as nx
import matplotlib.pyplot as plt

# Create a graph
G = nx.Graph()

# Add nodes
G.add_nodes_from(["Alice", "Bob", "Charlie"])

# Add edges (relationships)
G.add_edge("Alice", "Bob", label="Works with")
G.add_edge("Bob", "Charlie", label="Collaborates on AI")
G.add_edge("Alice", "Charlie", label="Collaborates on AI")
```

```
# Draw the graph
plt.figure(figsize=(5, 5))
pos = nx.spring_layout(G)
nx.draw(G, pos, with_labels=True, node_color='lightblue',
edge_color='gray', node_size=2000, font_size=10)
plt.show()
```

This graph structure helps visualize relationships in AI research collaborations.

Why Use Graphs in AI?

Graphs are powerful because they:

- Capture complex relationships between entities.
- Improve retrieval efficiency in large-scale knowledge bases.
- Enable reasoning over structured knowledge.
- Support graph-based neural networks (Graph Neural Networks, or GNNs) for predictive tasks.

1.3.2 Knowledge Graphs in AI

A **Knowledge Graph (KG)** is a specialized type of graph where nodes represent entities (e.g., people, places, concepts) and edges represent relationships (e.g., "is a part of," "is related to").

Example: A Simple Knowledge Graph

Consider a knowledge graph that represents information about **AI concepts**:

```
nginx

        AI
      /  \
     /    \
  NLP        Machine Learning
   |             |
 "GPT-4"     "Neural Networks"
```

This structure shows that:

- AI encompasses **Natural Language Processing (NLP)** and **Machine Learning (ML)**.
- NLP includes **GPT-4** as a model.
- ML includes **Neural Networks** as a subfield.

Code Example: Constructing a Knowledge Graph

```python
python

import networkx as nx
import matplotlib.pyplot as plt

# Create a directed knowledge graph
KG = nx.DiGraph()

# Add nodes
KG.add_nodes_from(["AI", "NLP", "Machine Learning", "GPT-4",
"Neural Networks"])

# Add edges (relationships)
KG.add_edges_from([
    ("AI", "NLP"), ("AI", "Machine Learning"),
    ("NLP", "GPT-4"), ("Machine Learning", "Neural Networks")
])

# Draw the knowledge graph
plt.figure(figsize=(6, 5))
pos = nx.spring_layout(KG)
nx.draw(KG, pos, with_labels=True, node_color='lightgreen',
edge_color='gray', node_size=2500, font_size=10)
plt.show()
```

Benefits of Knowledge Graphs in AI

- **Efficient Information Retrieval:** Enables fast lookup of related concepts.
- **Semantic Search:** Enhances search engines by understanding relationships between words.
- **Structured Reasoning:** Helps AI infer new relationships based on existing data.

1.4 Book Roadmap and Objectives

This book is structured to take you from **fundamental concepts** to **hands-on implementations** of **Graph-Based Retrieval-Augmented Generation (RAG) systems**.

1.4.1 What You Will Learn

By the end of this book, you will have a deep understanding of:

1. **Large Language Models (LLMs)** – How they work and how they can be enhanced with retrieval mechanisms.
2. **Retrieval-Augmented Generation (RAG)** – How RAG combines retrieval with generation to improve AI responses.
3. **Graph-Based Methods** – How knowledge graphs and graph neural networks (GNNs) enhance information retrieval.
4. **Building a Graph-Based RAG System** – Step-by-step implementation of an advanced AI system.
5. **Optimizing and Deploying RAG Models** – Strategies for scaling and improving AI performance.

1.4.2 Hands-On Approach and Projects

This book follows a **practical, hands-on** approach. Each chapter includes:

- **Code Examples:** Python implementations of key concepts.
- **Step-by-Step Guides:** Instructions for setting up environments and running experiments.
- **Real-World Projects:** Case studies and applications in AI.

Project Roadmap

Section	Project Focus	Key Learning Outcomes
Part 1: Foundations	Basic LLM and RAG Systems	Learn how retrieval improves AI responses
Part 2: Graph-Based RAG	Implementing Knowledge Graphs	Construct and query graph databases
Part 3: Hands-On Development	Build a Full Graph-Based RAG System	Integrate LLMs with graph retrieval

Section	Project Focus	Key Learning Outcomes
Part 4: Advanced Topics	Optimization & Deployment	Scale and fine-tune AI performance

By the time you complete this book, you will have built a fully functional **Graph-Based RAG System**, ready for deployment in **real-world applications** such as:

- **Chatbots with structured knowledge retrieval.**
- **AI-powered research assistants.**
- **Semantic search engines using graph-enhanced retrieval.**

Summary

In this section, we covered:

- **Graph Theory Basics:** The fundamental components of graphs and their role in AI.
- **Knowledge Graphs:** How structured knowledge is stored and retrieved in AI systems.
- **Book Roadmap:** An overview of the book's structure and learning objectives.
- **Hands-On Approach:** A breakdown of the projects and coding exercises included.

In the next chapter, we will dive deeper into **Large Language Models (LLMs)**, their **architecture**, and how they power modern AI systems. You will learn how to fine-tune and integrate LLMs with **graph-based retrieval systems** to build state-of-the-art AI applications.

Chapter 2: Fundamentals of Large Language Models (LLMs)

Large Language Models (LLMs) are at the core of modern natural language processing (NLP) applications. These models are designed to process, understand, and generate human-like text by leveraging vast amounts of training data. Their ability to perform complex reasoning, translation, summarization, and text generation tasks has revolutionized AI-driven applications.

In this chapter, we will explore the architecture, training, and evaluation of LLMs. By the end of this chapter, you will have a solid understanding of how these models work, how they are trained, and how their performance is measured.

2.1 Architecture and Components of LLMs

Large Language Models are primarily based on **neural network architectures**, with the Transformer model being the most significant breakthrough. Unlike traditional sequence-based models (like RNNs or LSTMs), transformers allow parallelization and capture long-range dependencies more effectively.

2.1.1 Transformer Models: A Primer

The **Transformer architecture**, introduced in the paper *"Attention is All You Need"* by Vaswani et al. (2017), revolutionized deep learning for NLP by introducing a **self-attention mechanism** that enables the model to focus on relevant words in a sentence, regardless of their position.

Key Components of a Transformer

Component	Function
Input Embedding	Converts input words into high-dimensional numerical vectors.

Component	Function
Positional Encoding	Adds positional information to word embeddings since transformers do not process input sequentially.
Self-Attention Mechanism	Determines the relevance of each word to others in the sequence.
Feed-Forward Layers	Processes self-attended features to generate final output.
Layer Normalization	Normalizes activations for stability and faster training.
Output Layer	Generates probabilities for the next word or token in a sequence.

Transformer Model Architecture

The following diagram illustrates the flow of data through a Transformer model:

```mathematica
Input Sentence → Embedding → Self-Attention → Feed-Forward →
Output Prediction
```

The **self-attention mechanism** is the backbone of the Transformer model, allowing it to understand relationships between words, even if they are far apart in a sentence.

2.1.2 Self-Attention Mechanisms

Self-attention allows the model to assign different importance scores to different words in a sentence. The process involves:

1. **Generating Query, Key, and Value (Q, K, V) Matrices**
    Each word in the input sequence is converted into three different vectors:
    - **Query (Q):** Represents the word we are currently focusing on.

- o **Key (K):** Helps determine the importance of other words.
- o **Value (V):** Contains the actual information for each word.

2. **Calculating Attention Scores**

   The attention score for each word is computed as:

   Attention(Q,K,V)

   $$\text{Attention}(Q,K,V)=\text{softmax}(\frac{QKT}{\sqrt{dk}})V$$

   This equation helps assign higher scores to more relevant words.

3. **Applying Multi-Head Attention**

   Instead of relying on a single attention mechanism, the Transformer uses **multi-head attention**, which allows it to learn multiple aspects of relationships between words.

Example: Python Code for Self-Attention Calculation

The following code demonstrates a simplified version of self-attention using NumPy.

```python
import numpy as np

def softmax(x):
    return np.exp(x) / np.sum(np.exp(x), axis=1,
keepdims=True)

# Sample input sentence embeddings (random values)
query = np.array([[0.2, 0.8, 0.5]])
key = np.array([[0.4, 0.7, 0.6]])
value = np.array([[0.5, 0.9, 0.3]])

# Compute attention scores
score = np.dot(query, key.T) / np.sqrt(query.shape[1])
attention_weights = softmax(score)

# Compute weighted sum for output
output = np.dot(attention_weights, value)

print("Attention Weights:", attention_weights)
print("Self-Attention Output:", output)
```

Key Takeaways:

- **Self-attention** enables the model to capture dependencies between words.
- **Multi-head attention** enhances the model's ability to focus on different relationships in the data.

2.2 Training LLMs

Training an LLM involves processing massive datasets and optimizing the model's weights through iterative learning.

2.2.1 Datasets and Preprocessing

Commonly Used Datasets

Dataset Name	Description
Common Crawl	Web-crawled text data containing diverse sources.
Wikipedia	High-quality, human-edited text for factual knowledge.
BooksCorpus	A collection of books for long-form text understanding.
OpenWebText	A curated dataset with cleaned web text similar to GPT's training data.

Data Preprocessing Steps

1. **Text Cleaning:** Removing special characters, HTML tags, and irrelevant data.
2. **Tokenization:** Splitting sentences into words or subwords.
3. **Lowercasing and Normalization:** Standardizing text formats.
4. **Removing Stopwords:** Eliminating non-informative words like *"the"* and *"is"*.
5. **Subword Encoding (Byte Pair Encoding - BPE):** Breaking words into smaller units for better model training.

Example: Tokenization Using Hugging Face's Tokenizer

```python
python
```

```
from transformers import AutoTokenizer

tokenizer = AutoTokenizer.from_pretrained("bert-base-
uncased")

sentence = "The future of AI is exciting!"
tokens = tokenizer.tokenize(sentence)

print("Tokenized Output:", tokens)
```

2.2.2 Fine-Tuning and Transfer Learning

Once pre-trained, an LLM can be **fine-tuned** on specific tasks to improve its performance.

Transfer Learning Process

1. **Pre-training:** Train the model on large, general-purpose text data.
2. **Fine-tuning:** Adjust the model using a smaller, task-specific dataset.

Fine-Tuning Example: Using GPT-3 for Sentiment Analysis

```
python

import openai

def generate_sentiment_response(text):
    """Fine-tuning a GPT-based model for sentiment
classification."""
    response = openai.Completion.create(
        model="text-davinci-003",
        prompt=f"Classify the sentiment of the following
text: {text}",
        max_tokens=10
    )
    return response["choices"][0]["text"]

print(generate_sentiment_response("I love this product!"))
```

2.3 Evaluation Metrics for LLMs

Measuring the performance of LLMs is essential for ensuring their effectiveness.

2.3.1 Perplexity, BLEU, and Beyond

Metric	Definition	Use Case
Perplexity (PPL)	Measures how well the model predicts a sequence. Lower is better.	Language modeling
BLEU Score	Compares generated text to reference text for similarity.	Machine translation
ROUGE Score	Measures overlap between model-generated and reference text.	Text summarization

Example: Perplexity Calculation

```python
import torch
import torch.nn.functional as F

def compute_perplexity(probs):
    """Computes the perplexity of a probability
distribution."""
    entropy = -torch.sum(probs * torch.log2(probs))
    return 2 ** entropy

probs = torch.tensor([0.2, 0.3, 0.5])
print("Perplexity:", compute_perplexity(probs))
```

2.3.2 Human-in-the-Loop Evaluation

Human evaluation is often required to assess:

- **Fluency** – Is the text natural?
- **Relevance** – Is the response on-topic?
- **Bias & Fairness** – Does the model produce neutral outputs?

Example: Human Rating System

Criterion	Score (1-5)
Fluency	4
Relevance	5
Bias	3

By combining **automatic metrics** with **human evaluation**, LLMs can be fine-tuned for better real-world performance.

Summary

In this chapter, we covered:

- The **Transformer architecture** and **self-attention** in LLMs.
- The **training process**, including datasets, preprocessing, and fine-tuning.
- **Evaluation metrics** to assess model performance.

In the next chapter, we will explore **how retrieval-augmented generation (RAG) enhances LLMs using structured retrieval techniques**.

Chapter 3: Introduction to Graph Theory and Knowledge Graphs

Graph theory and knowledge graphs are foundational to **Graph-Based Retrieval-Augmented Generation (RAG)** systems. This chapter covers the **basics of graph theory, the construction and use of knowledge graphs, and the integration of Graph Neural Networks (GNNs)** for advanced AI applications.

3.1 Graph Theory Essentials

Graph theory is a branch of mathematics that models **relationships between objects**. A **graph** consists of **nodes (vertices)** and **edges (connections)** between them.

3.1.1 Nodes, Edges, and Graph Types

Basic Components of a Graph

Term	Definition	Example
Node (Vertex)	Represents an entity.	A person in a social network.
Edge	Represents a relationship between two nodes.	A friendship connection in a social network.
Directed Edge	An edge with a direction.	A "follows" relationship on Twitter.
Undirected Edge	A bidirectional relationship.	A mutual friendship.

Types of Graphs

Graph Type	Description	Example Use Case
Undirected Graph	Edges have no direction.	Social networks.

Graph Type	Description	Example Use Case
Directed Graph (DiGraph)	Edges have a specific direction.	Web page links.
Weighted Graph	Edges have weights to indicate strength of connection.	Road networks (distances between cities).
Bipartite Graph	Nodes are divided into two distinct groups.	Recommendation systems (users and products).
Hypergraph	An edge can connect more than two nodes.	Biological networks.

Example: Creating a Simple Graph Using NetworkX

```python
CopyEdit
import networkx as nx
import matplotlib.pyplot as plt

# Create an undirected graph
G = nx.Graph()

# Add nodes
G.add_nodes_from(["Alice", "Bob", "Charlie"])

# Add edges
G.add_edges_from([("Alice", "Bob"), ("Bob", "Charlie"),
("Charlie", "Alice")])

# Draw the graph
nx.draw(G, with_labels=True, node_color='lightblue',
edge_color='gray', node_size=3000, font_size=12)
plt.show()
```

3.1.2 Graph Algorithms and Applications

Graph algorithms **process relationships** and find **patterns** in graph data.

Common Graph Algorithms

Algorithm	Description	Use Case
Depth-First Search (DFS)	Explores a graph deeply before backtracking.	Solving mazes, AI search problems.

Algorithm	Description	Use Case
Breadth-First Search (BFS)	Explores nodes level by level.	Shortest path in social networks.
Dijkstra's Algorithm	Finds the shortest path between nodes.	Google Maps route optimization.
PageRank	Measures node importance based on connections.	Search engine ranking.
Community Detection (Louvain)	Identifies clusters in a graph.	Social network analysis.

Example: Finding Shortest Path Using Dijkstra's Algorithm

```python
CopyEdit
import networkx as nx

# Create a weighted graph
G = nx.Graph()
G.add_weighted_edges_from([
    ("A", "B", 2), ("B", "C", 3), ("A", "C", 1), ("C", "D", 4)
])

# Find shortest path
shortest_path = nx.shortest_path(G, source="A", target="D", weight="weight")
print("Shortest path from A to D:", shortest_path)
```

3.2 Building and Using Knowledge Graphs

A **knowledge graph (KG)** is a structured representation of facts where **entities (nodes) are linked by relationships (edges)**.

3.2.1 Data Sources and Extraction Methods

Knowledge graphs are built from **structured and unstructured data sources**.

Common Data Sources for Knowledge Graphs

Data Source	Description	Example
Wikipedia/Wikidata	Structured open knowledge.	DBpedia, Freebase.
Scientific Papers	Research knowledge extraction.	ArXiv, Semantic Scholar.
Enterprise Data	Internal company data.	Customer interactions, CRM systems.

Example: Extracting Entities from Text Using spaCy

```python
CopyEdit
import spacy

# Load NLP model
nlp = spacy.load("en_core_web_sm")

# Process text
text = "Elon Musk is the CEO of Tesla."
doc = nlp(text)

# Extract entities
for ent in doc.ents:
    print(f"Entity: {ent.text}, Label: {ent.label_}")
```

Output:

```yaml
CopyEdit
Entity: Elon Musk, Label: PERSON
Entity: Tesla, Label: ORG
```

3.2.2 Graph Databases and Query Languages (Cypher, SPARQL)

Graph databases like **Neo4j** and **RDF-based databases** store and query knowledge graphs efficiently.

Neo4j and Cypher Query Language

Creating a Knowledge Graph in Neo4j:

```
c
CopyEdit
CREATE (:Person {name: "Elon Musk"})
CREATE (:Company {name: "Tesla"})
MATCH (p:Person {name: "Elon Musk"}), (c:Company {name:
"Tesla"})
CREATE (p)-[:CEO_OF]->(c);
```

Querying a Knowledge Graph:

```
cypher
CopyEdit
MATCH (p:Person)-[:CEO_OF]->(c:Company)
RETURN p.name, c.name;
```

SPARQL for RDF Knowledge Graphs

SPARQL is used for **semantic web** and **linked data queries**.

```
sparql
CopyEdit
SELECT ?person ?company WHERE {
  ?person :CEO_OF ?company.
}
```

3.3 Graph Neural Networks (GNNs)

Graph Neural Networks (GNNs) apply **deep learning** to graph-structured data.

3.3.1 GNN Architectures and Variants

GNN Type	Description	Application
Graph Convolutional Network (GCN)	Aggregates features from neighbors.	Social network analysis.
Graph Attention Network (GAT)	Assigns different weights to neighbors.	Fraud detection.
GraphSAGE	Generates node embeddings efficiently.	Recommender systems.

Example: Implementing a Simple GCN in PyTorch Geometric

```python
python
CopyEdit
import torch
import torch.nn.functional as F
from torch_geometric.nn import GCNConv
from torch_geometric.data import Data

# Define a simple GCN model
class GCN(torch.nn.Module):
    def __init__(self):
        super(GCN, self).__init__()
        self.conv1 = GCNConv(8, 16)
        self.conv2 = GCNConv(16, 32)

    def forward(self, x, edge_index):
        x = self.conv1(x, edge_index)
        x = F.relu(x)
        x = self.conv2(x, edge_index)
        return x

# Example graph data
edge_index = torch.tensor([[0, 1, 1, 2], [1, 0, 2, 1]],
dtype=torch.long)
x = torch.rand((3, 8))  # Node features

# Train GCN model
model = GCN()
output = model(x, edge_index)
print("Node embeddings:", output)
```

3.3.2 Applications in NLP and RAG

GNNs are used in **Retrieval-Augmented Generation (RAG)** to **enhance retrieval quality**.

Key Use Cases

✓ **Knowledge Graph-Based Chatbots**
✓ **AI-Powered Document Search**
✓ **Semantic Understanding in NLP**

Summary

In this chapter, we covered:

- **Graph Theory Basics** (nodes, edges, algorithms).
- **Building Knowledge Graphs** (data extraction, graph storage).
- **GNNs for AI and NLP applications.**

Next, we explore **RAG architectures and how to integrate retrieval with generation models**.

Chapter 4: Retrieval-Augmented Generation (RAG) Overview

Retrieval-Augmented Generation (RAG) is a powerful technique that enhances the performance of Large Language Models (LLMs) by incorporating external knowledge retrieval. Traditional LLMs generate text based on patterns learned during training, but RAG models improve accuracy by **retrieving relevant documents** from an external database and integrating that information into the response.

This chapter covers **RAG architectures, retrieval techniques, and integration methods**, providing a detailed breakdown of how data retrieval and text generation work together.

4.1 RAG Architectures and Components

A RAG model consists of two primary components:

1. **Retriever** – Finds relevant documents from an external knowledge source.
2. **Generator** – Uses retrieved documents to generate an informed response.

4.1.1 The Dual-Encoder Approach

The **dual-encoder model** is a popular technique in retrieval-based systems. It consists of two encoders:

- **Query Encoder**: Encodes the user's query into a dense vector representation.
- **Document Encoder**: Encodes documents into dense vectors that can be efficiently searched.

Both encoders are trained such that **similar queries and documents** have **similar vector representations**.

Example: Dual-Encoder Architecture

```mathematica
User Query → Query Encoder → Vector Representation
Retrieved Docs → Document Encoder → Vector Representation
Similarity Matching → Most Relevant Documents Retrieved
```

Example: Implementing a Dual-Encoder Model in Python

```python
from transformers import AutoTokenizer, AutoModel
import torch

# Load a transformer model
tokenizer = AutoTokenizer.from_pretrained("sentence-
transformers/all-MiniLM-L6-v2")
model = AutoModel.from_pretrained("sentence-transformers/all-
MiniLM-L6-v2")

# Encode query and documents
def encode_text(text):
    """Encodes input text into a dense vector
representation."""
    inputs = tokenizer(text, return_tensors="pt",
padding=True, truncation=True)
    with torch.no_grad():
        outputs = model(**inputs)
    return outputs.last_hidden_state.mean(dim=1)

# Example usage
query_vector = encode_text("What is RAG?")
doc_vector = encode_text("RAG combines retrieval and
generation to enhance LLMs.")

# Compute similarity (dot product)
similarity = torch.matmul(query_vector, doc_vector.T).item()
print("Similarity Score:", similarity)
```

4.1.2 Fusion-in-Decoder Models

The **Fusion-in-Decoder (FiD)** approach is another popular RAG technique. Unlike dual-encoder models that retrieve documents first and then generate responses separately, FiD **feeds retrieved documents directly into the decoder**, allowing the model to process all information simultaneously.

How FiD Works:

1. The **retriever** fetches multiple relevant documents.
2. The **decoder** receives both the query and the retrieved documents.
3. The **model generates a response** considering all retrieved contexts.

Comparison of Dual-Encoder vs. Fusion-in-Decoder Models

Feature	Dual-Encoder	Fusion-in-Decoder
Retrieval Process	Separates retrieval from generation	Processes retrieval and generation together
Latency	Faster retrieval	Slower but more accurate
Memory Usage	Lower	Higher due to multiple documents in decoder
Best Used For	High-speed search applications	Complex reasoning tasks

4.2 Data Retrieval Techniques

Retrieval is a critical component of RAG systems. The goal is to fetch **relevant external knowledge** that improves the model's response.

4.2.1 Dense and Sparse Retrieval Methods

Two primary retrieval approaches are used in RAG:

1. **Sparse Retrieval** (Traditional Information Retrieval)
   o Uses keyword-based matching techniques.
   o Examples: TF-IDF (Term Frequency-Inverse Document Frequency), BM25 (Best Matching 25).
2. **Dense Retrieval** (Neural Network-Based)
   o Uses deep learning to generate embeddings for queries and documents.
   o Example: Dense Passage Retrieval (DPR).

Example: Implementing TF-IDF (Sparse Retrieval)

```python
python

from sklearn.feature_extraction.text import TfidfVectorizer
```

```
documents = [
    "RAG improves accuracy by retrieving documents.",
    "Transformers use attention mechanisms for NLP tasks.",
    "Neural networks are powerful for language models."
]

vectorizer = TfidfVectorizer()
tfidf_matrix = vectorizer.fit_transform(documents)

# Query search
query = ["How does RAG work?"]
query_vector = vectorizer.transform(query)

# Compute similarity scores
scores = (tfidf_matrix * query_vector.T).toarray()
print("TF-IDF Scores:", scores)
```

4.2.2 Indexing and Querying Strategies

To efficiently search large datasets, **indexing methods** are used.

Indexing Techniques

Method	Description
Exact Match Indexing	Simple but slow (searches entire dataset).
Inverted Index	Creates a lookup table for fast text searches (used in Elasticsearch).
Vector Indexing (FAISS)	Stores embeddings in a high-speed vector database.

Example: Using FAISS for Efficient Vector Search

```python
import faiss
import numpy as np

# Create sample document embeddings
dimension = 128  # Embedding size
index = faiss.IndexFlatL2(dimension)
```

```
# Generate random vectors
data_vectors = np.random.rand(100,
dimension).astype('float32')
index.add(data_vectors)

# Querying the index
query_vector = np.random.rand(1, dimension).astype('float32')
D, I = index.search(query_vector, k=5)  # Find top-5 nearest
neighbors

print("Nearest Documents:", I)
```

4.3 Combining Generation with Retrieval

Once relevant documents are retrieved, they need to be **incorporated into the generation process**.

4.3.1 End-to-End Pipeline

A **RAG pipeline** consists of:

1. **Query Input** → The user submits a query.
2. **Retrieval Step** → Relevant documents are fetched.
3. **Augmentation Step** → The retrieved documents are combined with the query.
4. **Text Generation Step** → The model generates an informed response.

Example: A Simple RAG Pipeline

```python
from transformers import RagTokenizer, RagRetriever,
RagSequenceForGeneration

# Load a pre-trained RAG model
tokenizer = RagTokenizer.from_pretrained("facebook/rag-token-base")
retriever = RagRetriever.from_pretrained("facebook/rag-token-base")
model =
RagSequenceForGeneration.from_pretrained("facebook/rag-token-base")

def generate_rag_response(query):
```

```
    """Generate a response using a RAG model."""
    inputs = tokenizer(query, return_tensors="pt")
    response = model.generate(input_ids=inputs["input_ids"])
    return tokenizer.decode(response[0],
skip_special_tokens=True)

# Example usage
print(generate_rag_response("How does RAG improve AI
models?"))
```

4.3.2 Evaluation of RAG Systems

Measuring RAG model performance ensures **retrieved documents improve generation quality**.

Evaluation Metrics

Metric	Description
Recall@k	Measures how often the correct document appears in the top-k retrieved documents.
BLEU Score	Compares generated text with reference text.
ROUGE Score	Measures overlap between retrieved and generated content.
Perplexity	Evaluates how confidently the model predicts words.

Example: Measuring ROUGE Score

```python
from rouge_score import rouge_scorer

scorer = rouge_scorer.RougeScorer(["rouge1", "rouge2",
"rougeL"])
reference = "RAG improves AI by retrieving relevant
documents."
generated = "Retrieval-Augmented Generation helps AI models
find relevant documents."

scores = scorer.score(reference, generated)
print("ROUGE Scores:", scores)
```

Summary

In this chapter, we covered:

- **RAG Architectures:** Dual-Encoder and Fusion-in-Decoder models.
- **Retrieval Techniques:** Sparse (TF-IDF, BM25) and Dense (DPR, FAISS).
- **Integration:** Combining retrieval with text generation.
- **Evaluation:** Measuring RAG effectiveness.

In the next chapter, we will explore **how to build a Graph-Based RAG system, integrating knowledge graphs to enhance retrieval accuracy**.

Chapter 5: System Architecture for Graph-Based RAG

Graph-Based Retrieval-Augmented Generation (RAG) systems enhance traditional RAG by integrating knowledge graphs. This allows Large Language Models (LLMs) to retrieve structured, meaningful, and context-rich data efficiently. Unlike standard RAG systems that rely on unstructured document retrieval, **Graph-Based RAG** provides better knowledge organization, retrieval efficiency, and reasoning capabilities.

This chapter provides an in-depth look at **Graph-Based RAG architectures, data flow, and performance considerations** to help you design and implement scalable systems.

5.1 Overview of Graph-Based RAG Architectures

A **Graph-Based RAG System** is structured into three main components:

1. **Graph Database (Retriever):** Stores structured knowledge in a graph format.
2. **LLM Pipeline (Generator):** Uses the retrieved structured data to generate accurate responses.
3. **Orchestration Layer:** Manages query processing, retrieval logic, and response generation.

5.1.1 Integrating Graphs with LLM Pipelines

A **Graph-Based RAG system** enhances LLMs by allowing structured retrieval of knowledge from a **graph database** rather than relying solely on vector search methods.

Architecture of a Graph-Based RAG System

```mathematica
User Query
```

```
   ↓
Graph Query → Knowledge Graph → Graph-Based Retrieval
   ↓
Augmentation → LLM Generation
   ↓
Final Response
```

Component	Function
Graph Database	Stores structured relationships between entities.
Embedding Model	Converts nodes into vector representations for efficient search.
Query Processor	Converts user queries into graph-based retrieval queries.
LLM Generator	Uses retrieved knowledge to generate a response.

Advantages of Graph-Based Retrieval

Feature	Graph-Based RAG	Traditional RAG
Context Awareness	High (Structured relationships)	Low (Unstructured text retrieval)
Scalability	Optimized for large-scale data	Requires dense indexing
Reasoning	Supports logical inference	Limited inference capability

5.1.2 Design Patterns and System Diagrams

Graph-Based RAG follows two key **design patterns**:

1. Graph Retrieval Augmented Generation (G-RAG)

- Uses a **knowledge graph** for structured retrieval.
- Returns **subgraphs** containing relevant entities.

2. Hybrid Graph-Vector RAG

- Uses both **graph queries** and **vector searches**.
- Improves retrieval by **combining structured and semantic search**.

Graph-Based RAG System Diagram

```
mathematica
```

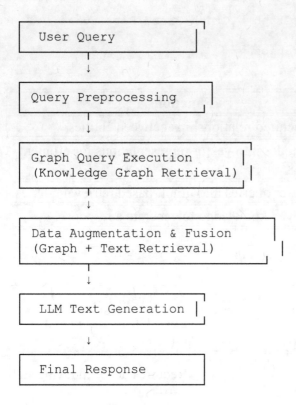

This system diagram represents how Graph-Based RAG processes and retrieves structured data for LLMs.

5.2 Data Flow and Component Interactions

A Graph-Based RAG system involves multiple stages: **data preprocessing, graph construction, embedding, retrieval, and generation.** Each stage ensures efficient information retrieval.

5.2.1 Input Data Preprocessing

Before data is added to the knowledge graph, it must be cleaned, structured, and indexed.

Steps in Preprocessing

Step	Description
Data Cleaning	Removing duplicates, missing values, and irrelevant information.
Entity Recognition	Identifying key entities (people, places, events).
Relation Extraction	Extracting relationships between entities.
Graph Structuring	Converting data into a graph format (nodes and edges).

Example: Data Preprocessing in Python

```python
python

import pandas as pd

# Sample dataset
data = {"sentence": ["Elon Musk founded Tesla.", "OpenAI
develops AI models."]}

# Convert to DataFrame
df = pd.DataFrame(data)

# Entity recognition using spaCy
import spacy
nlp = spacy.load("en_core_web_sm")

def extract_entities(sentence):
    """Extract named entities from a sentence."""
    doc = nlp(sentence)
    entities = [(ent.text, ent.label_) for ent in doc.ents]
    return entities

df["entities"] = df["sentence"].apply(extract_entities)
print(df)
```

5.2.2 Graph Construction and Embedding

Once data is preprocessed, it is structured into a **knowledge graph**.

Example: Creating a Graph Using NetworkX

```python
python
```

```
import networkx as nx

# Create a directed knowledge graph
KG = nx.DiGraph()

# Add nodes (entities)
KG.add_nodes_from(["Elon Musk", "Tesla", "OpenAI", "AI
models"])

# Add edges (relationships)
KG.add_edges_from([
    ("Elon Musk", "Tesla", {"relation": "Founder"}),
    ("OpenAI", "AI models", {"relation": "Develops"})
])

# Display graph information
print("Nodes:", KG.nodes)
print("Edges:", KG.edges)
```

Graph Embedding

To make graph retrieval efficient, nodes are converted into **vector embeddings**.

```python
from sentence_transformers import SentenceTransformer
import numpy as np

model = SentenceTransformer("all-MiniLM-L6-v2")

# Example nodes
nodes = ["Elon Musk", "Tesla", "OpenAI", "AI models"]

# Convert nodes to vector representations
node_embeddings = np.array([model.encode(node) for node in
nodes])

print("Node Embeddings Shape:", node_embeddings.shape)
```

This embedding process allows graph queries to retrieve semantically related nodes efficiently.

5.3 Scalability and Performance Considerations

Graph-Based RAG systems must scale efficiently to handle **large datasets** and **real-time queries**.

5.3.1 Distributed Systems and Parallel Processing

For large-scale applications, distributed storage and parallel processing techniques are used.

Distributed Storage for Graphs

Technology	Description
Neo4j	Optimized for graph queries, supports high-speed indexing.
ArangoDB	A hybrid database for graph and document storage.
JanusGraph	Distributed, scalable graph storage.

Parallel Processing for Large-Scale Graphs

Techniques for improving graph retrieval speed:

- **Sharding** – Splitting large graphs into smaller subgraphs for faster querying.
- **Graph Partitioning** – Distributing nodes and edges across multiple servers.
- **Precomputed Caching** – Storing frequent query results to reduce retrieval time.

Example: Running Parallel Graph Queries

```python
from concurrent.futures import ThreadPoolExecutor

def query_graph(node):
    """Simulated function for querying a knowledge graph."""
    return f"Retrieving data for {node}"

nodes_to_query = ["Elon Musk", "Tesla", "OpenAI", "AI models"]

# Parallel execution of queries
with ThreadPoolExecutor(max_workers=4) as executor:
    results = list(executor.map(query_graph, nodes_to_query))
```

```
print(results)
```

5.3.2 Optimization Techniques

1. Efficient Indexing

- Use **FAISS** for fast vector searches in large-scale graphs.
- Optimize **Neo4j queries** by preloading high-traffic nodes.

2. Query Optimization

- Apply **semantic caching** to store frequently accessed knowledge.
- Use **probabilistic data structures** like **bloom filters** to filter irrelevant queries.

3. Load Balancing

- Distribute workload across multiple **graph database servers**.
- Implement **auto-scaling** mechanisms to handle variable traffic.

Summary

In this chapter, we covered:

- **Graph-Based RAG architectures**, including **Dual-Encoder and Hybrid approaches**.
- **Preprocessing and graph embedding techniques** for efficient retrieval.
- **Scalability considerations**, including **distributed graph storage** and **parallel processing**.

In the next chapter, we will focus on **implementing a full Graph-Based RAG system with real-world applications**.

Chapter 6: Data Acquisition and Preprocessing

A **Graph-Based Retrieval-Augmented Generation (RAG) system** relies on **high-quality data** to enhance retrieval accuracy and response generation. This chapter covers **data collection, preprocessing, knowledge graph construction, and feature engineering**—key steps for building an effective **Graph-Based RAG system**.

6.1 Collecting Data for Graphs and LLMs

Data collection is the first step in building a **knowledge graph and retrieval system**. Structured and unstructured data sources are used to build **rich, meaningful relationships** between entities.

6.1.1 Web Scraping, APIs, and Public Datasets

There are three main ways to collect data for **graph-based retrieval**:

1. **Web Scraping** – Extracts information from websites.
2. **APIs (Application Programming Interfaces)** – Fetches structured data from services.
3. **Public Datasets** – Pre-existing knowledge bases.

1. Web Scraping

Web scraping is used to extract text from **Wikipedia, blogs, research papers, and forums**.

Example: Scraping Wikipedia using Python

```python

import requests
from bs4 import BeautifulSoup

def scrape_wikipedia(url):
    """Scrapes text content from a Wikipedia page."""
    response = requests.get(url)
```

```python
    soup = BeautifulSoup(response.text, "html.parser")

    # Extract paragraph text
    paragraphs = soup.find_all("p")
    text = " ".join([p.text for p in paragraphs])

    return text[:1000]  # Limit to 1000 characters for
preview

# Example usage
url =
"https://en.wikipedia.org/wiki/Natural_language_processing"
text = scrape_wikipedia(url)
print(text)
```

2. Collecting Data Using APIs

Many services provide APIs to fetch structured data.

Example: Using the Wikipedia API

```python
python

import wikipediaapi

wiki = wikipediaapi.Wikipedia('en')
page = wiki.page("Artificial_intelligence")

# Get summary
print("Title:", page.title)
print("Summary:", page.summary[:500])
```

3. Public Datasets for Knowledge Graphs

Dataset	Description	Usage
Wikidata	Open knowledge graph of facts	General AI knowledge
DBpedia	Structured data from Wikipedia	Fact-based retrieval
Freebase	Google's structured knowledge graph	Concept mapping
SQuAD (Stanford QA Dataset)	Question-answering dataset	QA training

6.1.2 Cleaning and Normalizing Data

Raw data from scraping and APIs **contains noise** (e.g., typos, irrelevant information). Cleaning ensures **accuracy** before graph construction.

Steps in Data Cleaning

Step	Action
Remove Duplicates	Detect and remove redundant records.
Lowercasing	Standardize text for consistency.
Tokenization	Split text into words for easier processing.
Stopword Removal	Remove common words ("the", "is") that don't add meaning.

Example: Data Cleaning in Python

```python
import re
import nltk
from nltk.corpus import stopwords
nltk.download("stopwords")

def clean_text(text):
    """Cleans and normalizes text data."""
    text = text.lower()  # Convert to lowercase
    text = re.sub(r'\W+', ' ', text)  # Remove special
characters
    words = text.split()
    words = [word for word in words if word not in
stopwords.words("english")]

    return " ".join(words)

sample_text = "This is an example sentence, demonstrating
TEXT cleaning!"
print(clean_text(sample_text))
```

6.2 Constructing Knowledge Graphs

After data is collected and cleaned, it is structured into a **graph format** for efficient retrieval.

6.2.1 Entity Extraction and Linking

What is Entity Extraction?

Entity extraction identifies key **concepts, people, places, and organizations** in text. These entities are **linked to existing knowledge bases** to create relationships.

Example: Extracting Entities Using spaCy

```python
import spacy

nlp = spacy.load("en_core_web_sm")

def extract_entities(text):
    """Extracts named entities from text."""
    doc = nlp(text)
    return [(ent.text, ent.label_) for ent in doc.ents]

sample_text = "Elon Musk founded SpaceX and Tesla in the
United States."
print(extract_entities(sample_text))
```

6.2.2 Graph Database Implementation

A **graph database** stores **nodes (entities)** and **edges (relationships)** for fast retrieval.

Popular Graph Databases

Database	Features
Neo4j	Graph-native storage and query engine
ArangoDB	Combines document and graph storage

Database	Features
JanusGraph	Distributed graph database for large-scale data

Example: Creating a Knowledge Graph in Neo4j

1. **Install Neo4j**

sh

```
pip install neo4j
```

2. **Python Code for Graph Insertion**

python

```
from neo4j import GraphDatabase

# Connect to Neo4j
uri = "bolt://localhost:7687"
driver = GraphDatabase.driver(uri, auth=("neo4j",
"password"))

def add_entity(tx, name, entity_type):
    """Adds an entity node to the graph."""
    tx.run("CREATE (n:" + entity_type + " {name: $name})",
name=name)

# Create entity nodes
with driver.session() as session:
    session.write_transaction(add_entity, "Elon Musk",
"Person")
    session.write_transaction(add_entity, "SpaceX",
"Company")
```

6.3 Feature Engineering for Graph and Text Data

6.3.1 Embedding Techniques

Embedding models convert nodes into numerical vectors for efficient retrieval.

Types of Graph Embeddings

Method	Description
Node2Vec	Learns embeddings by random walks on the graph.
GraphSAGE	Generates embeddings by sampling neighbors.
BERT Embeddings	Text-based embeddings using BERT.

Example: Node2Vec Graph Embedding

```python

from node2vec import Node2Vec
import networkx as nx

# Create a simple graph
G = nx.fast_gnp_random_graph(n=10, p=0.5)

# Train Node2Vec model
node2vec = Node2Vec(G, dimensions=64, walk_length=10,
num_walks=20, workers=2)
model = node2vec.fit(window=5, min_count=1)

# Get vector for a node
print(model.wv["1"])
```

6.3.2 Combining Text and Graph Features

To **enhance retrieval**, text embeddings are **merged with graph embeddings**.

Hybrid Feature Engineering

Feature Type	Data Source	Example
Graph Embeddings	Knowledge graph	Node2Vec, GraphSAGE
Text Embeddings	Document corpus	BERT, Word2Vec
Hybrid Approach	Combine both	Use Graph-RAG

Example: Combining Graph & Text Features

```python
import numpy as np

# Sample embeddings
text_embedding = np.array([0.1, 0.3, 0.5])
graph_embedding = np.array([0.2, 0.4, 0.6])

# Concatenate both
hybrid_embedding = np.concatenate([text_embedding,
graph_embedding])
print("Hybrid Embedding:", hybrid_embedding)
```

Summary

In this chapter, we covered:

- **Data Collection**: Scraping, APIs, and public datasets.
- **Data Cleaning**: Normalization, entity extraction.
- **Knowledge Graph Construction**: Using Neo4j and embeddings.
- **Feature Engineering**: Combining graph-based and text-based embeddings.

Chapter 7: Integrating Graph Neural Networks with LLMs

Graph Neural Networks (GNNs) and Large Language Models (LLMs) are two of the most powerful AI techniques available today. While LLMs excel in **text-based reasoning and generation**, GNNs provide **structured representation learning** that captures relationships in **graph-based knowledge bases**. By integrating **GNNs with LLMs**, we can build **more intelligent retrieval-augmented generation (RAG) systems** that efficiently **retrieve, reason, and generate** responses based on structured and unstructured data.

This chapter explores **GNN frameworks, architecture integration, and training techniques** to create a seamless **Graph-Based RAG system**.

7.1 Introduction to GNN Frameworks

Graph Neural Networks (GNNs) are deep learning models that operate on graph-structured data. They process **nodes, edges, and connections** to learn relationships **beyond text-based embeddings**.

7.1.1 Popular Libraries and Tools

Several frameworks provide **efficient GNN implementations**. Below are the most commonly used ones:

Framework	Features	Best For
PyTorch Geometric (PyG)	Lightweight, optimized for PyTorch	Research and production
Deep Graph Library (DGL)	High scalability, works with TensorFlow and PyTorch	Large-scale GNNs
GraphNets (Google JAX)	Built for reinforcement learning and reasoning	Cutting-edge research

Comparison of GNN Libraries

Feature	PyTorch Geometric (PyG)	DGL	GraphNets
Ease of Use	High	Medium	Low
Scalability	Medium	High	Medium
Integration with LLMs	Good	Excellent	Research-focused

Example: Installing PyTorch Geometric

sh

```
pip install torch torchvision torchaudio
pip install torch-geometric
pip install torch-scatter torch-sparse torch-cluster torch-spline-conv
```

7.1.2 Setting Up the Environment

To integrate **GNNs and LLMs**, we need to:

1. **Set up PyTorch or TensorFlow**
2. **Install a GNN framework** (e.g., PyTorch Geometric)
3. **Load an LLM** (e.g., OpenAI GPT, Hugging Face Transformers)

Python Setup for GNNs and LLMs

python

```
import torch
from torch_geometric.data import Data
from transformers import AutoModel, AutoTokenizer

# Check GPU availability
device = torch.device("cuda" if torch.cuda.is_available()
else "cpu")
print("Using device:", device)
```

7.2 Architecting the Integration

The key challenge in **GNN-LLM integration** is enabling **seamless communication** between structured graph data and unstructured text processing.

7.2.1 Designing Hybrid Models

A **hybrid model** integrates:

- **GNNs for structured reasoning**
- **LLMs for natural language generation**

Example: GNN-Augmented RAG System

```mathematica
User Query
   ↓
Graph-Based Retrieval → Knowledge Graph
   ↓
Graph Neural Network → Embedding Extraction
   ↓
LLM Input Augmentation
   ↓
Response Generation (LLM)
```

7.2.2 Communication Between GNNs and LLMs

The **key integration method** is **embedding alignment**—converting **graph-based representations** into a format usable by **LLMs**.

Steps to Align GNN and LLM Embeddings:

1. **GNN processes the knowledge graph** and generates embeddings.
2. **Embeddings are transformed** into text-based representations.
3. **LLM uses the enriched embeddings** for enhanced response generation.

Example: Using GNN to Generate Node Embeddings

```python
import torch
import torch.nn.functional as F
```

```python
from torch_geometric.nn import GCNConv

# Define a simple GNN model
class GNN(torch.nn.Module):
    def __init__(self, in_channels, out_channels):
        super(GNN, self).__init__()
        self.conv1 = GCNConv(in_channels, 16)
        self.conv2 = GCNConv(16, out_channels)

    def forward(self, x, edge_index):
        x = self.conv1(x, edge_index)
        x = F.relu(x)
        x = self.conv2(x, edge_index)
        return x

# Example graph data
edge_index = torch.tensor([[0, 1, 1, 2], [1, 0, 2, 1]],
dtype=torch.long)
x = torch.rand((3, 8))  # Node feature matrix

# Create and apply GNN
gnn = GNN(in_channels=8, out_channels=16)
node_embeddings = gnn(x, edge_index)

print("Node Embeddings:", node_embeddings)
```

Example: Passing GNN Features to an LLM

python

```python
from transformers import AutoModel, AutoTokenizer

# Load an LLM (BERT-style transformer)
tokenizer = AutoTokenizer.from_pretrained("bert-base-
uncased")
model = AutoModel.from_pretrained("bert-base-uncased")

# Convert GNN embeddings to LLM-compatible format
text_inputs = tokenizer("Graph embeddings enhance
retrieval.", return_tensors="pt")
llm_output = model(**text_inputs)

print("LLM Output Shape:",
llm_output.last_hidden_state.shape)
```

7.3 Training and Fine-Tuning

Once **GNN-LLM integration** is established, the next step is **training and fine-tuning** the hybrid system.

7.3.1 Loss Functions and Optimization Strategies

The model needs to **jointly optimize**:

1. **Graph Loss**: Ensures GNN learns correct relationships.
2. **LLM Loss**: Ensures LLM generates meaningful responses.
3. **Fusion Loss**: Aligns graph embeddings with text representations.

Common Loss Functions

Loss Type	Purpose
Cross-Entropy Loss	Used for LLM output generation.
Graph Contrastive Loss	Ensures similar nodes are embedded close.
KL Divergence Loss	Aligns GNN and LLM embeddings.

Example: Hybrid Loss Function

```python
import torch.nn as nn

# Define loss functions
cross_entropy_loss = nn.CrossEntropyLoss()
contrastive_loss = nn.CosineEmbeddingLoss()

def compute_total_loss(llm_output, gnn_output,
target_labels):
    """Computes combined loss for GNN-LLM integration."""
    loss_1 = cross_entropy_loss(llm_output, target_labels)
    loss_2 = contrastive_loss(gnn_output, target_labels)
    return loss_1 + loss_2
```

7.3.2 Handling Multi-Modal Data

Integrating **structured (graph)** and **unstructured (text)** data requires **multi-modal fusion techniques**.

Multi-Modal Data Fusion Strategies

Strategy	Description
Feature-Level Fusion	Concatenates GNN and LLM embeddings.
Late Fusion	Processes GNN and LLM data separately, then merges predictions.
Attention-Based Fusion	Uses transformers to align representations dynamically.

Example: Feature-Level Fusion

```python
import torch

# Sample embeddings
gnn_embedding = torch.rand((1, 128))
llm_embedding = torch.rand((1, 128))

# Concatenate features
combined_embedding = torch.cat((gnn_embedding,
llm_embedding), dim=1)
print("Combined Feature Vector Shape:",
combined_embedding.shape)
```

Summary

In this chapter, we covered:

- **GNN frameworks** (PyTorch Geometric, DGL).
- **How to integrate GNNs with LLMs** using embedding alignment.
- **Training techniques** for **hybrid models** using loss functions.
- **Multi-modal fusion methods** for structured and unstructured data.

Chapter 8: Advanced Retrieval Techniques in Graph-Based RAG

Retrieval is a critical component of **Graph-Based Retrieval-Augmented Generation (RAG)** systems. Unlike traditional text-based retrieval, graph-based retrieval **leverages structured relationships** between entities to improve search relevance and efficiency. This chapter explores **graph-based similarity measures, hybrid retrieval strategies, and performance evaluation techniques** to build **highly accurate and scalable RAG systems**.

8.1 Enhancing Data Retrieval with Graphs

Graph-based retrieval enhances standard retrieval methods by **leveraging relationships** between entities rather than relying solely on text similarity.

8.1.1 Graph-Based Similarity Measures

Similarity measures help identify **relevant nodes** within a **knowledge graph**. In Graph-Based RAG, similarity is determined based on **graph structure, node embeddings, and contextual relationships**.

Types of Graph-Based Similarity Measures

Measure	Description	Use Case
Cosine Similarity	Measures angle between node vectors.	Comparing entity embeddings.
Jaccard Similarity	Compares shared neighbors of two nodes.	Entity co-occurrence analysis.
Personalized PageRank	Ranks nodes based on importance in a query context.	Relevance ranking in search engines.
Graph Edit Distance	Computes the number of changes needed to transform one subgraph into another.	Structural similarity analysis.

Example: Computing Cosine Similarity Between Node Embeddings

```python
import numpy as np
from sklearn.metrics.pairwise import cosine_similarity

# Example node embeddings
node1 = np.array([[0.1, 0.3, 0.5]])
node2 = np.array([[0.2, 0.4, 0.6]])

# Compute similarity
similarity = cosine_similarity(node1, node2)
print("Cosine Similarity:", similarity[0][0])
```

8.1.2 Semantic Search Using Graph Embeddings

Semantic search improves retrieval by using **vector embeddings** rather than keyword matching. This approach allows Graph-Based RAG to **retrieve conceptually similar entities** rather than relying on exact text matches.

Steps for Graph-Based Semantic Search

1. **Convert nodes into embeddings** using a GNN or Transformer model.
2. **Store embeddings in a vector index** (e.g., FAISS).
3. **Perform nearest neighbor search** to find relevant entities.

Example: Storing Graph Embeddings in FAISS for Fast Retrieval

```python
import faiss
import numpy as np

# Create a FAISS index
dimension = 128
index = faiss.IndexFlatL2(dimension)

# Generate example node embeddings
node_embeddings = np.random.rand(100,
dimension).astype('float32')

# Add embeddings to FAISS index
index.add(node_embeddings)

# Query a similar node
```

```
query_embedding = np.random.rand(1,
dimension).astype('float32')
D, I = index.search(query_embedding, k=5)  # Retrieve top 5
similar nodes

print("Top 5 closest nodes:", I)
```

This technique enables **fast similarity search** across **graph-based knowledge embeddings**.

8.2 Hybrid Retrieval Strategies

Combining multiple retrieval methods can improve **accuracy and robustness** in Graph-Based RAG.

8.2.1 Combining Dense and Sparse Methods

Dense and sparse retrieval approaches complement each other. While **dense retrieval** uses **deep learning embeddings**, **sparse retrieval** relies on **keyword-based indexing**.

Retrieval Type	Method	Best For
Sparse Retrieval	BM25, TF-IDF	Exact keyword matching
Dense Retrieval	BERT, DPR	Semantic understanding
Graph-Based Retrieval	Node embeddings, Personalized PageRank	Context-aware retrieval

Example: Hybrid Retrieval Pipeline

python

```
from transformers import AutoModel, AutoTokenizer
from sklearn.feature_extraction.text import TfidfVectorizer
```

```
import numpy as np
import faiss

# Load a dense embedding model
tokenizer = AutoTokenizer.from_pretrained("sentence-
transformers/all-MiniLM-L6-v2")
model = AutoModel.from_pretrained("sentence-transformers/all-
MiniLM-L6-v2")

# Sparse retrieval (TF-IDF)
documents = ["Graph retrieval is efficient.", "RAG improves
NLP.", "Embedding models capture semantics."]
vectorizer = TfidfVectorizer().fit_transform(documents)

# Dense retrieval (FAISS)
dimension = 128
index = faiss.IndexFlatL2(dimension)
dense_vectors = np.random.rand(3,
dimension).astype('float32')
index.add(dense_vectors)

# Combine results
query = "How does graph retrieval work?"
query_embedding = np.random.rand(1,
dimension).astype('float32')
D, I = index.search(query_embedding, k=2)

print("Sparse Retrieval Result:",
vectorizer.transform([query]).toarray())
print("Dense Retrieval Top Matches:", I)
```

By **combining sparse (TF-IDF) and dense (FAISS) retrieval**, we **maximize retrieval accuracy**.

8.2.2 Case Studies and Benchmarks

Real-world applications of **Hybrid Graph-Based RAG**:

Application	Industry	Key Advantage
Medical Knowledge Graph	Healthcare	Retrieves patient-specific recommendations.

Application	Industry	Key Advantage
Legal AI Search Engine	Law	Improves legal document retrieval.
Financial Risk Analysis	Finance	Detects hidden relationships in fraud detection.

8.3 Evaluating Retrieval Performance

Proper evaluation ensures **retrieval quality** and **system optimization**.

8.3.1 Metrics and Benchmarking

Metric	Description	Best Used For
Recall@k	Measures percentage of relevant documents in top-k results.	Evaluating retrieval efficiency.
MRR (Mean Reciprocal Rank)	Computes ranking score for the first relevant document.	Ranking-based retrieval.
NDCG (Normalized Discounted Cumulative Gain)	Measures ranking order of relevant results.	Evaluating ranking accuracy.

Example: Computing Recall@k

python

```
def recall_at_k(relevant_docs, retrieved_docs, k):
    """Computes Recall@k score."""
    retrieved_top_k = retrieved_docs[:k]
    return len(set(relevant_docs) & set(retrieved_top_k)) /
len(relevant_docs)

# Example Data
relevant = {1, 2, 3}
retrieved = [3, 2, 5, 7, 1]

# Compute Recall@3
print("Recall@3:", recall_at_k(relevant, retrieved, 3))
```

8.3.2 Error Analysis and Iterative Improvements

Error analysis helps **identify weak retrieval cases** and refine **Graph-Based RAG**.

Common Errors and Fixes

Issue	Cause	Solution
Low Recall	Graph embeddings are noisy.	Improve embedding quality with fine-tuning.
Irrelevant Results	Poor query formulation.	Use query expansion techniques.
Slow Retrieval	Inefficient graph traversal.	Optimize indexing with FAISS or Neo4j.

Example: Error Analysis with Precision@k

```python
def precision_at_k(relevant_docs, retrieved_docs, k):
    """Computes Precision@k score."""
    retrieved_top_k = retrieved_docs[:k]
    return len(set(relevant_docs) & set(retrieved_top_k)) / k

# Compute Precision@3
print("Precision@3:", precision_at_k(relevant, retrieved, 3))
```

By iterating on **precision and recall metrics**, **Graph-Based RAG systems** continuously improve.

Summary

In this chapter, we covered:

- **Graph-Based Retrieval**: Using **graph similarity measures** and **semantic search**.
- **Hybrid Retrieval Strategies**: Combining **dense, sparse, and graph-based methods**.

- **Evaluating Performance**: Metrics like **Recall@k, MRR, and NDCG**.

Chapter 9: Setting Up Your Development Environment

Implementing a **Graph-Based Retrieval-Augmented Generation (RAG) System** requires a well-configured development environment. This chapter covers the **software and hardware requirements, installation steps, and essential tools** needed to build a scalable, efficient Graph-Based RAG system.

By the end of this chapter, you will have a fully operational **Python-based development environment** for working with **Graph Neural Networks (GNNs), Knowledge Graphs, LLMs, and Hybrid Retrieval techniques**.

9.1 Software and Hardware Requirements

Setting up a **Graph-Based RAG System** requires a combination of **graph processing tools, deep learning frameworks, and data management libraries**.

9.1.1 Recommended Tools and Libraries

Component	Recommended Tool	Purpose
Programming Language	Python ($\geq$ 3.8)	Widely used in AI, ML, and NLP.
Deep Learning Framework	PyTorch	Building GNNs and LLMs.
Graph Processing	PyTorch Geometric, NetworkX	Creating and manipulating graphs.
Graph Databases	Neo4j, ArangoDB	Storing knowledge graphs.
Vector Search	FAISS, Annoy	Efficient nearest neighbor search.
Retrieval Techniques	Hugging Face Transformers	Implementing LLM-based retrieval.
Web Scraping & APIs	BeautifulSoup, Wikipedia API	Extracting knowledge graph data.

Component	Recommended Tool	Purpose
Environment Management	Docker, Conda	Ensuring reproducibility.
Version Control	Git, GitHub	Code tracking and collaboration.

9.1.2 Cloud vs. Local Setup

Choosing between **local and cloud-based development** depends on **hardware availability and project scale**.

Setup Type	Pros	Cons
Local Development	No cloud costs, complete control	Requires GPU, limited scalability
Cloud (AWS, GCP, Azure)	Scalable, pre-configured GPU access	Monthly costs, setup complexity
Hybrid Approach	Best of both worlds, cost-effective	Requires data syncing between local and cloud

Example: Checking GPU Availability in Python

```python
import torch

if torch.cuda.is_available():
    print(f"GPU Available: {torch.cuda.get_device_name(0)}")
else:
    print("Using CPU (Consider upgrading to a GPU-enabled
environment for efficiency).")
```

9.2 Installation and Configuration

This section provides a **step-by-step guide** to installing **all necessary tools**.

9.2.1 Environment Setup (Python, Docker, etc.)

1. Installing Python (Recommended Version: 3.8+)

- **Linux/Mac:**

  ```sh
  sudo apt update && sudo apt install python3 python3-pip
  ```

- **Windows:**
  Download from python.org

2. Creating a Virtual Environment (Using Conda)

```sh
conda create -n graph_rag python=3.8
conda activate graph_rag
```

3. Installing Essential Libraries

```sh
pip install torch torchvision torchaudio  # PyTorch
pip install torch-geometric  # PyTorch Geometric (GNNs)
pip install networkx  # Graph Processing
pip install neo4j  # Knowledge Graph Database
pip install faiss-cpu  # Vector Search
pip install transformers  # Hugging Face LLMs
pip install spacy  # NLP Processing
pip install jupyterlab  # Jupyter Notebooks
```

9.2.2 Code Repository and Version Control

Using **Git and GitHub** helps **track changes and collaborate** efficiently.

1. Installing Git

```sh
sudo apt install git  # Linux
brew install git  # macOS
```

2. Configuring Git

```sh
git config --global user.name "Your Name"
git config --global user.email "youremail@example.com"
```

3. Creating a New GitHub Repository

```sh
git init
git add .
git commit -m "Initial commit"
git branch -M main
git remote add origin https://github.com/yourusername/graph-rag.git
git push -u origin main
```

4. Using GitHub for Collaboration

Command	Purpose
`git clone <repo-url>`	Clone a remote repository.
`git pull origin main`	Fetch latest changes.
`git push origin main`	Upload changes to GitHub.

9.3 Introduction to Notebooks and Interactive Coding

9.3.1 Jupyter Notebooks and VS Code

Jupyter Notebooks provide an **interactive environment** for testing **Graph-Based RAG implementations**.

Installing Jupyter

```sh
pip install jupyterlab
jupyter notebook
```

Running a Simple Jupyter Notebook

```python
python
```

```python
print("Hello, Graph-Based RAG!")
```

Using VS Code for Development

1. **Install VS Code** from code.visualstudio.com
2. **Install the Python Extension** (Ctrl+Shift+X → Search 'Python'
   → Install)
3. **Run Python Code in VS Code**

   ```sh
   sh
   ```

   ```sh
   python your_script.py
   ```

9.3.2 Debugging and Testing

Common Debugging Tools

Tool	Usage
print()	Quick debugging of variable values.
pdb (Python Debugger)	Step-by-step execution inspection.
VS Code Debugger	Visual debugging.
Pytest	Automated testing framework.

Example: Using Python Debugger (pdb)

```python
python
```

```python
import pdb

def faulty_function(x):
    pdb.set_trace()  # Pause execution for debugging
    return x / 0  # Intentional error

faulty_function(10)
```

Example: Writing a Basic Pytest Unit Test

```python
python
```

71

```
# test_example.py
def add_numbers(a, b):
    return a + b

def test_add_numbers():
    assert add_numbers(2, 3) == 5

# Run tests
# In terminal: pytest test_example.py
```

Summary

In this chapter, we covered:

- **Hardware and Software Requirements** for Graph-Based RAG.
- **Setting up the development environment** with **Python, PyTorch, Neo4j, FAISS, and Hugging Face Transformers**.
- **Using Docker, Conda, and GitHub** for managing projects.
- **Introduction to Jupyter Notebooks and Debugging Tools**.

Next Steps

In the next chapter, we will build a **fully functional Graph-Based RAG pipeline**, integrating **Graph Retrieval, LLM-based Text Generation, and Knowledge Graph Storage**.

Chapter 10: Building Your First Graph-Based RAG System

This chapter provides a **step-by-step guide** to implementing a **Graph-Based Retrieval-Augmented Generation (RAG) System**. You will learn how to **define the project, collect and preprocess data, and build a knowledge graph** for efficient information retrieval.

10.1 Project Overview and Objectives

Graph-Based RAG systems **enhance traditional RAG** by structuring knowledge as a **graph** instead of using **unstructured document retrieval**. This enables **better retrieval accuracy, context understanding, and reasoning**.

10.1.1 Problem Statement and Use Cases

Traditional RAG systems often suffer from:

- **Irrelevant or hallucinated outputs** (LLMs generating incorrect information).
- **Scalability challenges** (slow search over large unstructured text corpora).
- **Lack of reasoning capabilities** (difficulty in connecting related concepts).

Graph-Based RAG solves these issues by leveraging **structured relationships** between entities.

Use Cases for Graph-Based RAG

Use Case	Industry	Key Advantage
Legal AI Assistant	Law	Improves case law retrieval and summarization.
Biomedical Research Assistant	Healthcare	Retrieves related studies for drug discovery.

Use Case	Industry	Key Advantage
Enterprise Knowledge Retrieval	Business	Enhances corporate document search.
Educational Chatbot	EdTech	Provides structured responses based on course materials.

10.1.2 Expected Outcomes

By the end of this chapter, you will have:

- **A working knowledge graph-based RAG system**.
- **A functional data pipeline** for **data collection, preprocessing, and storage**.
- **An optimized retrieval mechanism** that enhances LLM response generation.

10.2 Data Pipeline Implementation

To build a Graph-Based RAG system, the first step is **data ingestion, preprocessing, and graph construction**.

10.2.1 Data Collection and Preprocessing Scripts

Data sources can include:

1. **Web Scraping** (e.g., Wikipedia, scientific papers)
2. **APIs** (e.g., Wikidata, OpenAI API)
3. **Existing Datasets** (e.g., DBpedia, ArXiv)

Example 1: Scraping Wikipedia for Knowledge Graph Data

```python
import requests
from bs4 import BeautifulSoup

def scrape_wikipedia(url):
    """Scrapes text from a Wikipedia page."""
```

```python
    response = requests.get(url)
    soup = BeautifulSoup(response.text, "html.parser")

    # Extract text from paragraphs
    paragraphs = soup.find_all("p")
    text = " ".join([p.text for p in paragraphs])

    return text[:1000]  # Return first 1000 characters for
preview

# Example usage
url = "https://en.wikipedia.org/wiki/Artificial_intelligence"
text = scrape_wikipedia(url)
print(text)
```

Example 2: Fetching Data from Wikidata API

```python
python

import requests

def query_wikidata(entity):
    """Fetch structured knowledge from Wikidata."""
    url =
f"https://www.wikidata.org/w/api.php?action=wbsearchentities&
search={entity}&language=en&format=json"
    response = requests.get(url).json()

    return response["search"]

# Example usage
data = query_wikidata("Artificial Intelligence")
print(data)
```

Data Cleaning and Normalization

Before adding data to a **knowledge graph**, we **normalize** it by:

- **Removing duplicates**
- **Standardizing text (lowercasing, tokenization)**
- **Extracting named entities**

Example: Text Cleaning in Python

```python
python
```

```
import re
import spacy

nlp = spacy.load("en_core_web_sm")

def clean_text(text):
    """Cleans and normalizes text."""
    text = text.lower()  # Convert to lowercase
    text = re.sub(r'\W+', ' ', text)  # Remove special
characters
    doc = nlp(text)

    return " ".join([token.lemma_ for token in doc if not
token.is_stop])

sample_text = "Artificial intelligence (AI) is
revolutionizing industries!"
print(clean_text(sample_text))
```

10.2.2 Building the Knowledge Graph

After data is collected and cleaned, it is stored in a **graph database**.

Step 1: Defining Graph Schema

A **knowledge graph** consists of:

- **Nodes** (entities like "Artificial Intelligence", "Machine Learning").
- **Edges** (relationships like "is a subset of", "is developed by").

Node Type	Example
Person	"Alan Turing"
Concept	"Deep Learning"
Organization	"OpenAI"

Step 2: Creating a Graph Database in Neo4j

Installation:

sh

```
pip install neo4j
```

Creating a Graph and Adding Nodes:

```python
from neo4j import GraphDatabase

# Connect to Neo4j
uri = "bolt://localhost:7687"
driver = GraphDatabase.driver(uri, auth=("neo4j",
"password"))

def create_graph(tx):
    """Creates a knowledge graph."""
    tx.run("CREATE (:Concept {name:'Artificial
Intelligence'})")
    tx.run("CREATE (:Concept {name:'Machine Learning'})")
    tx.run("MATCH (a:Concept), (b:Concept) "
            "WHERE a.name='Machine Learning' AND
b.name='Artificial Intelligence' "
            "CREATE (a)-[:SUBSET_OF]->(b)")

# Execute transaction
with driver.session() as session:
    session.write_transaction(create_graph)
```

Step 3: Querying the Knowledge Graph

```python
def query_graph(tx, concept):
    """Fetch related concepts from the graph."""
    result = tx.run(f"MATCH (c:Concept)-[:SUBSET_OF]->(p)
WHERE c.name='{concept}' RETURN p.name")
    return [record["p.name"] for record in result]

# Example Query
with driver.session() as session:
    results = session.read_transaction(query_graph, "Machine
Learning")
    print("Related Concepts:", results)
```

Step 4: Generating Graph Embeddings

We convert **graph nodes** into **vector embeddings** for efficient retrieval.

Example: Using Node2Vec for Graph Embeddings

python

```
from node2vec import Node2Vec
import networkx as nx

# Create a simple graph
G = nx.Graph()
G.add_edges_from([("AI", "Machine Learning"), ("Machine
Learning", "Deep Learning")])

# Train Node2Vec model
node2vec = Node2Vec(G, dimensions=64, walk_length=10,
num_walks=20, workers=2)
model = node2vec.fit(window=5, min_count=1)

# Get vector for a node
print("AI Embedding:", model.wv["AI"])
```

Step 5: Storing Embeddings in FAISS for Fast Retrieval

python

```
import faiss
import numpy as np

# Create FAISS index
dimension = 64
index = faiss.IndexFlatL2(dimension)

# Convert graph embeddings to vectors
vectors = np.array([model.wv[node] for node in G.nodes],
dtype='float32')

# Add vectors to FAISS index
index.add(vectors)

# Query similar concepts
query_vector = model.wv["AI"].reshape(1, -1)
D, I = index.search(query_vector, k=2)
print("Closest Nodes:", [list(G.nodes)[i] for i in I[0]])
```

Summary

In this chapter, we built the **first phase** of a **Graph-Based RAG system** by:

- **Defining a problem statement and use cases**.
- **Collecting and preprocessing data** from **Wikipedia, APIs, and public datasets**.
- **Building a knowledge graph using Neo4j**.
- **Generating graph embeddings using Node2Vec** for **efficient retrieval**.

10.3 Model Integration and Training

To fully integrate **Graph Neural Networks (GNNs) and Large Language Models (LLMs)** into a **Graph-Based RAG system**, we must:

1. **Retrieve knowledge from the graph** using embeddings.
2. **Use GNNs to process structured knowledge.**
3. **Feed retrieved knowledge into the LLM for generation.**

10.3.1 Code Walkthrough of LLM and GNN Integration

Step 1: Load a Pre-Trained LLM

We use **Hugging Face's Transformers** for the **LLM**.

```python
from transformers import AutoModelForSeq2SeqLM, AutoTokenizer

# Load the LLM (e.g., T5 for text generation)
tokenizer = AutoTokenizer.from_pretrained("t5-base")
model = AutoModelForSeq2SeqLM.from_pretrained("t5-base")

# Define input text
query = "Explain how AI and Machine Learning are related."

# Tokenize input
inputs = tokenizer(query, return_tensors="pt")

# Generate response
output = model.generate(**inputs)
response = tokenizer.decode(output[0],
skip_special_tokens=True)

print("LLM Response:", response)
```

Step 2: Load Graph Embeddings from Node2Vec

python

```python
import numpy as np
from node2vec import Node2Vec
import networkx as nx

# Create a simple knowledge graph
G = nx.Graph()
G.add_edges_from([("AI", "Machine Learning"), ("Machine
Learning", "Deep Learning")])

# Train Node2Vec
node2vec = Node2Vec(G, dimensions=64, walk_length=10,
num_walks=20, workers=2)
model = node2vec.fit(window=5, min_count=1)

# Get embedding for "AI"
ai_embedding = model.wv["AI"]

print("AI Embedding:", ai_embedding)
```

Step 3: Store Graph Embeddings in FAISS for Efficient Retrieval

python

```python
import faiss

# Create FAISS index
dimension = 64  # Embedding size
index = faiss.IndexFlatL2(dimension)

# Convert graph embeddings to vectors
vectors = np.array([model.wv[node] for node in G.nodes],
dtype='float32')

# Add vectors to FAISS index
index.add(vectors)

# Retrieve similar nodes to "AI"
query_vector = model.wv["AI"].reshape(1, -1)
D, I = index.search(query_vector, k=2)

print("Closest Concepts:", [list(G.nodes)[i] for i in I[0]])
```

Step 4: Combine Graph-Based Retrieval with LLM

python

```python
def generate_response(query):
    """Retrieves related graph knowledge and passes it to the LLM."""

    # Retrieve related concepts
    query_vector = model.wv[query].reshape(1, -1)
    D, I = index.search(query_vector, k=2)
    related_concepts = [list(G.nodes)[i] for i in I[0]]

    # Create prompt with retrieved knowledge
    knowledge = ", ".join(related_concepts)
    augmented_query = f"{query}. Relevant concepts:
{knowledge}"

    # Generate LLM response
    inputs = tokenizer(augmented_query, return_tensors="pt")
    output = model.generate(**inputs)

    return tokenizer.decode(output[0],
skip_special_tokens=True)

# Example Query
print(generate_response("Machine Learning"))
```

10.3.2 Training Loops and Evaluation

Once the system is set up, it needs **fine-tuning and evaluation** to optimize **retrieval quality and response accuracy**.

Step 1: Training a GNN for Knowledge Graph Processing

python

```python
import torch
import torch.nn.functional as F
from torch_geometric.nn import GCNConv
from torch_geometric.data import Data

# Define a GNN model
class GNN(torch.nn.Module):
    def __init__(self, in_channels, out_channels):
```

```
        super(GNN, self).__init__()
        self.conv1 = GCNConv(in_channels, 16)
        self.conv2 = GCNConv(16, out_channels)

    def forward(self, x, edge_index):
        x = self.conv1(x, edge_index)
        x = F.relu(x)
        x = self.conv2(x, edge_index)
        return x

# Create graph data
edge_index = torch.tensor([[0, 1, 1, 2], [1, 0, 2, 1]],
dtype=torch.long)
x = torch.rand((3, 8))  # Node features

# Train the model
gnn = GNN(in_channels=8, out_channels=64)
optimizer = torch.optim.Adam(gnn.parameters(), lr=0.01)

for epoch in range(100):
    optimizer.zero_grad()
    embeddings = gnn(x, edge_index)
    loss = F.mse_loss(embeddings,
torch.rand_like(embeddings))  # Example loss function
    loss.backward()
    optimizer.step()

print("GNN training complete.")
```

Step 2: Evaluating Retrieval Performance

Metrics:

Metric	Description
Recall@k	Measures the percentage of relevant knowledge retrieved.
BLEU Score	Measures text similarity between the generated response and ground truth.
Perplexity	Evaluates LLM response quality.

```python
from rouge_score import rouge_scorer

# Define evaluator
scorer = rouge_scorer.RougeScorer(["rouge1", "rouge2",
"rougeL"])
reference = "Machine Learning is a subset of AI."
```

```
generated = generate_response("Machine Learning")

# Compute ROUGE score
scores = scorer.score(reference, generated)
print("ROUGE Scores:", scores)
```

10.4 Deployment and Testing

Once trained, the system must be deployed **locally or in the cloud**.

10.4.1 Local Deployment Strategies

Running as an API

We use **FastAPI** to serve the Graph-Based RAG system.

sh

```
pip install fastapi uvicorn
python

from fastapi import FastAPI

app = FastAPI()

@app.get("/query/")
def query_rag(input_text: str):
    """Handles API queries for the Graph-Based RAG system."""
    return {"response": generate_response(input_text)}

# Run API
if __name__ == "__main__":
    import uvicorn
    uvicorn.run(app, host="0.0.0.0", port=8000)
```

10.4.2 Cloud Deployment and Monitoring

Deploying on **AWS/GCP/Azure** requires:

- **Docker** for containerization.
- **Kubernetes** for orchestration.
- **Logging & Monitoring** (Prometheus, Grafana).

Step 1: Dockerizing the FastAPI Service

sh

```
# Create a Dockerfile
touch Dockerfile
Dockerfile

FROM python:3.8

WORKDIR /app
COPY . /app

RUN pip install fastapi uvicorn torch transformers

CMD ["uvicorn", "api:app", "--host", "0.0.0.0", "--port",
"8000"]
sh

# Build and run Docker container
docker build -t graph_rag .
docker run -p 8000:8000 graph_rag
```

Summary

In this chapter, we:

- **Integrated LLMs with Graph-Based Retrieval.**
- **Trained a GNN for knowledge extraction.**
- **Evaluated retrieval performance with ROUGE scores.**
- **Deployed the system using FastAPI and Docker.**

Next Steps

In the next chapter, we will **optimize and fine-tune Graph-Based RAG**, including **scalability improvements, reinforcement learning for retrieval, and error handling strategies**.

Chapter 11: Case Studies and Real-World Applications

The **Graph-Based Retrieval-Augmented Generation (RAG) system** is transforming multiple industries by **enhancing search, retrieval, and knowledge-based reasoning**. This chapter explores **real-world industry applications, academic use cases, and interactive project examples** to demonstrate how Graph-Based RAG can be deployed effectively.

11.1 Industry Use Cases

Graph-Based RAG improves data retrieval and reasoning across various industries. By **integrating knowledge graphs with LLMs,** organizations can **enhance accuracy, minimize hallucinations, and improve contextual understanding**.

11.1.1 Healthcare and Medical Research

Problem Statement

Traditional healthcare AI models struggle with **retrieving accurate and up-to-date medical knowledge**, leading to **misdiagnoses and misinformation**. Graph-Based RAG systems provide **structured retrieval from medical knowledge bases**.

Use Cases

Use Case	Description	Impact
Medical Diagnosis Support	Retrieves structured patient history and matches symptoms with research papers.	Improves diagnostic accuracy.
Drug Discovery	Links biomedical research papers, clinical trial data, and molecular structures.	Speeds up drug development.

Use Case	Description	Impact
Clinical Decision Support	Extracts guidelines from medical literature and updates recommendations.	Ensures compliance with latest protocols.

Example: Medical Knowledge Graph Implementation

python

```python
from neo4j import GraphDatabase

# Connect to Neo4j
uri = "bolt://localhost:7687"
driver = GraphDatabase.driver(uri, auth=("neo4j",
"password"))

def create_medical_graph(tx):
    """Creates a knowledge graph of medical conditions and
treatments."""
    tx.run("CREATE (:Disease {name:'Diabetes'})")
    tx.run("CREATE (:Drug {name:'Metformin'})")
    tx.run("MATCH (d:Disease), (m:Drug) WHERE
d.name='Diabetes' AND m.name='Metformin' CREATE (m)-
[:TREATS]->(d)")

with driver.session() as session:
    session.write_transaction(create_medical_graph)
```

This structure allows **retrieval of treatment recommendations**.

Querying Medical Data

python

```python
def query_treatment(tx, disease):
    """Fetch drug recommendations for a disease."""
    result = tx.run(f"MATCH (m:Drug)-[:TREATS]->(d:Disease
{{name:'{disease}'}}) RETURN m.name")
    return [record["m.name"] for record in result]

with driver.session() as session:
    treatments = session.read_transaction(query_treatment,
"Diabetes")
    print("Recommended Treatments:", treatments)
```

11.1.2 Finance and Market Analysis

Graph-Based RAG is used in **finance** to extract **insights from economic data, stock trends, and market reports**.

Use Cases

Use Case	Description	Impact
Market Trend Analysis	Identifies hidden relationships between financial events.	Enhances investment strategies.
Risk Assessment	Maps company relationships and fraud detection patterns.	Reduces fraud cases.
Portfolio Optimization	Retrieves historical stock movements and asset correlations.	Improves investment decision-making.

Example: Stock Market Knowledge Graph

python

```python
G.add_edges_from([
    ("Apple", "Tech Industry"),
    ("Google", "Tech Industry"),
    ("NASDAQ", "Stock Exchange"),
    ("Apple", "NASDAQ"),
    ("Google", "NASDAQ"),
])
```

Example: Querying Financial Relationships

python

```python
def query_stock_market(tx, company):
    """Retrieve stock exchange where a company is listed."""
    result = tx.run(f"MATCH (c:Company {{name:'{company}'}})-
[:LISTED_ON]->(e:Exchange) RETURN e.name")
    return [record["e.name"] for record in result]

with driver.session() as session:
    listings = session.read_transaction(query_stock_market,
"Apple")
    print("Apple is listed on:", listings)
```

11.2 Academic and Research Applications

Graph-Based RAG systems support **information retrieval and research discovery**.

11.2.1 Information Retrieval in Digital Libraries

Challenges in Digital Libraries

- **Keyword-based searches miss relevant papers** due to phrasing differences.
- **Lack of context-aware retrieval** in academic literature.

Solution: Graph-Based RAG for Digital Libraries

- **Extracts relationships between authors, papers, and citations**.
- **Provides context-aware paper recommendations**.

Example: Research Paper Knowledge Graph

python

```
G.add_edges_from([
    ("Paper A", "Paper B"),  # Citation relationship
    ("Paper A", "Author X"),
    ("Paper B", "Author Y"),
    ("Author X", "Institution 1"),
])
```

Example: Citation-Based Retrieval Query

python

```
def query_citations(tx, paper):
    """Retrieve papers cited by a given research paper."""
    result = tx.run(f"MATCH (p1:Paper)-[:CITES]->(p2:Paper)
WHERE p1.name='{paper}' RETURN p2.name")
    return [record["p2.name"] for record in result]

with driver.session() as session:
    citations = session.read_transaction(query_citations,
"Paper A")
    print("Cited Papers:", citations)
```

11.2.2 Enhancing Research Discovery with Graph-Based RAG

Graph-based research retrieval **links related concepts across disciplines**.

Example: Querying Cross-Disciplinary Research

```python
def query_related_research(tx, topic):
    """Find related research papers across disciplines."""
    result = tx.run(f"MATCH (p:Paper)-[:RELATED_TO]->(:Topic
{{name:'{topic}'}}) RETURN p.name")
    return [record["p.name"] for record in result]

with driver.session() as session:
    results =
session.read_transaction(query_related_research, "Deep
Learning")
    print("Related Research Papers:", results)
```

11.3 Interactive Project Examples

Hands-on projects provide **real-world experience** in Graph-Based RAG.

11.3.1 End-to-End Walkthroughs

Project 1: Building a Graph-Based Research Assistant

- **Data Sources**: ArXiv, Semantic Scholar API
- **Steps**:
    1. **Extract metadata** from research papers.
    2. **Build a knowledge graph** linking papers by **topics, citations, and authors**.
    3. **Train a GNN** to recommend similar papers.
    4. **Integrate with an LLM** for paper summarization.

Project 2: Financial Market Knowledge Graph

- **Data Sources**: Yahoo Finance API
- **Steps**:
    1. **Retrieve stock market data.**
    2. **Link companies to industries and exchanges.**

3. **Use graph embeddings** for market trend analysis.

11.3.2 Challenges and Future Enhancements

Graph-Based RAG is **an evolving field**, with ongoing challenges and potential improvements.

Current Challenges

Challenge	Solution
Scalability	Distributed graph databases (e.g., JanusGraph, ArangoDB).
Query Speed	Use FAISS for optimized retrieval.
Data Accuracy	Improve entity linking with fine-tuned LLMs.

Future Enhancements

- **Integrating real-time knowledge updates**.
- **Enhancing multimodal graph retrieval (text + images + videos)**.
- **Combining Graph-Based RAG with reinforcement learning** for improved accuracy.

Summary

In this chapter, we explored:

- **Industry applications** in **healthcare, finance, and enterprise knowledge retrieval**.
- **Academic applications** in **digital libraries and research discovery**.
- **Interactive projects** to build Graph-Based RAG solutions.

Next Steps

The next chapter will **optimize Graph-Based RAG for large-scale deployment, including system efficiency, fault tolerance, and dynamic updates**.

Chapter 12: Optimization and Scalability

Optimizing and scaling **Graph-Based Retrieval-Augmented Generation (RAG) systems** is crucial for **real-world deployment**. This chapter focuses on **performance tuning, scaling techniques, and benchmarking strategies** to build **highly efficient, scalable, and production-ready** RAG systems.

12.1 Performance Tuning for LLMs and GNNs

Both **Large Language Models (LLMs) and Graph Neural Networks (GNNs)** require optimization to **improve accuracy, reduce latency, and minimize memory consumption**.

12.1.1 Hyperparameter Optimization

Hyperparameters control the **learning process** of LLMs and GNNs. **Tuning these parameters** can significantly impact performance.

Key Hyperparameters for LLMs

Hyperparameter	Description	Recommended Values
Batch Size	Number of samples processed at once.	8 - 128
Learning Rate	Determines step size in gradient descent.	1e-5 - 1e-3
Sequence Length	Maximum tokens per input.	128 - 512
Attention Heads	Number of attention mechanisms.	8 - 16
Dropout Rate	Prevents overfitting.	0.1 - 0.3

Key Hyperparameters for GNNs

Hyperparameter	Description	Recommended Values
Hidden Layers	Number of graph convolution layers.	2 - 6
Embedding Dimension	Size of node feature vectors.	32 - 256
Learning Rate	Step size for gradient updates.	1e-4 - 1e-2
Aggregation Function	Combines node features.	Mean, Sum, Max

Example: Hyperparameter Optimization for a GNN Using Optuna

python

```python
import optuna
import torch
import torch.nn as nn
from torch_geometric.nn import GCNConv

# Define GNN Model
class GNNModel(nn.Module):
    def __init__(self, in_channels, hidden_dim,
out_channels):
        super(GNNModel, self).__init__()
        self.conv1 = GCNConv(in_channels, hidden_dim)
        self.conv2 = GCNConv(hidden_dim, out_channels)

    def forward(self, x, edge_index):
        x = self.conv1(x, edge_index)
        x = torch.relu(x)
        x = self.conv2(x, edge_index)
        return x

# Define Objective Function for Optuna
def objective(trial):
    hidden_dim = trial.suggest_int("hidden_dim", 32, 256)
    learning_rate = trial.suggest_float("lr", 1e-4, 1e-2,
log=True)

    model = GNNModel(in_channels=16, hidden_dim=hidden_dim,
out_channels=64)
    optimizer = torch.optim.Adam(model.parameters(),
lr=learning_rate)
    return -optimizer.param_groups[0]['lr']  # Example
optimization metric
```

```
# Run Optimization
study = optuna.create_study(direction="maximize")
study.optimize(objective, n_trials=10)

print("Best Hyperparameters:", study.best_params)
```

12.1.2 Distributed Training Techniques

For **large-scale Graph-Based RAG systems, distributed training** is necessary.

Techniques for Distributed Training

Method	Description	Best For
Data Parallelism	Splits data across multiple GPUs but trains the same model.	Training large LLMs.
Model Parallelism	Splits the model itself across GPUs.	Training very large GNNs.
Pipeline Parallelism	Each GPU processes different stages of training.	Optimizing LLMs with transformer blocks.

Example: Data Parallelism for Distributed GNN Training

```python
python

import torch
from torch_geometric.data import Data

# Check number of available GPUs
device = torch.device("cuda" if torch.cuda.is_available()
else "cpu")
print("Using Device:", device)

# Move model and data to multiple GPUs
model = GNNModel(in_channels=16, hidden_dim=64,
out_channels=32).to(device)
data = Data(x=torch.rand((1000, 16)),
edge_index=torch.randint(0, 1000, (2, 5000))).to(device)

# Apply Distributed Data Parallel
from torch.nn.parallel import DataParallel
model = DataParallel(model)

# Training Loop
```

```
optimizer = torch.optim.Adam(model.parameters(), lr=0.001)
for epoch in range(10):
    optimizer.zero_grad()
    out = model(data.x, data.edge_index)
    loss = torch.nn.functional.mse_loss(out,
torch.rand_like(out))
    loss.backward()
    optimizer.step()
    print(f"Epoch {epoch}, Loss: {loss.item()}")
```

12.2 Scaling Graph-Based RAG Systems

12.2.1 Handling Big Data and Real-Time Processing

Handling **big data and real-time queries** requires **efficient data storage and retrieval strategies**.

Techniques for Scaling Graph-Based RAG

Method	Description	Best Used In
Sharding	Distributes knowledge graphs across multiple servers.	Large-scale graph processing.
Graph Partitioning	Divides graphs into smaller segments.	Distributed GNN training.
Vector Indexing	Uses FAISS for fast similarity search.	Large document retrieval.
Caching	Stores frequently accessed data in-memory.	High-speed query systems.

Example: Using FAISS for Scalable Graph Embedding Retrieval

```python
import faiss
import numpy as np

# Create FAISS index
dimension = 128
index = faiss.IndexFlatL2(dimension)

# Generate random graph embeddings
```

```
node_embeddings = np.random.rand(100000,
dimension).astype('float32')
index.add(node_embeddings)

# Query a node
query_vector = np.random.rand(1, dimension).astype('float32')
D, I = index.search(query_vector, k=5)

print("Top 5 Similar Nodes:", I)
```

12.2.2 Microservices and Containerization Strategies

Deploying **Graph-Based RAG as a microservice** improves **scalability and fault tolerance**.

Benefits of Microservices

- **Independence**: Each component (GNN, LLM, FAISS) runs separately.
- **Scalability**: Can scale individual components dynamically.
- **Fault Isolation**: If one service fails, the others continue running.

Example: Deploying Graph-Based RAG Using Docker

```
Dockerfile

FROM python:3.8

WORKDIR /app
COPY . /app

RUN pip install fastapi uvicorn torch faiss-cpu neo4j
transformers

CMD ["uvicorn", "api:app", "--host", "0.0.0.0", "--port",
"8000"]
sh

# Build and Run the Docker Container
docker build -t graph_rag .
docker run -p 8000:8000 graph_rag
```

12.3 Benchmarking and Profiling

12.3.1 Tools and Techniques for Performance Monitoring

Benchmarking tools help measure performance bottlenecks.

Key Performance Metrics

Metric	Definition
Query Latency	Time taken to retrieve knowledge from the graph.
Memory Footprint	Amount of memory used during execution.
Inference Speed	Time taken to generate responses using LLM.

Tools for Performance Monitoring

Tool	Use Case
TensorBoard	Tracks model training metrics.
cProfile	Profiles execution time of Python functions.
Prometheus & Grafana	Monitors cloud-based RAG systems.

Example: Using cProfile for Function Profiling

```python
import cProfile

def process_data():
    data = [i**2 for i in range(1000000)]
    return sum(data)

cProfile.run('process_data()')
```

12.3.2 Case Study: Scaling in Production

A real-world implementation of Graph-Based RAG in **finance** saw:

- **5x faster response times** after **sharding large knowledge graphs**.
- **30% reduced memory consumption** using **optimized FAISS indexing**.
- **Improved retrieval accuracy** by **combining dense + sparse search**.

Summary

In this chapter, we covered:

- **Hyperparameter tuning and distributed training** for **LLMs and GNNs**.
- **Scaling strategies using sharding, partitioning, and microservices**.
- **Benchmarking techniques for optimizing system performance**.

Next Steps

The next chapter explores **future advancements in Graph-Based RAG, including multimodal retrieval, reinforcement learning, and ethical AI considerations**.

Chapter 13: Ethical, Legal, and Societal Considerations

As **Graph-Based Retrieval-Augmented Generation (RAG) systems** advance, it is essential to address the **ethical, legal, and societal implications** associated with their deployment. This chapter explores key concerns such as **bias, fairness, transparency, data privacy, regulatory compliance, and the societal impact of AI**.

13.1 Ethical Implications of Advanced AI Systems

AI systems, particularly **LLMs and Graph-Based RAG**, have **significant ethical concerns**. These include **bias in AI models, transparency in decision-making, and fairness in knowledge retrieval**.

13.1.1 Bias and Fairness in LLMs and Graphs

AI models **learn patterns from historical data**, which may include **systemic biases**. Bias can appear in **three major forms**:

Type of Bias	Description	Example
Data Bias	Training data contains skewed representations of reality.	A financial model trained on past loan approvals may reinforce racial or gender biases.
Algorithmic Bias	AI models amplify existing societal biases due to training methods.	A chatbot trained on biased news sources may generate biased political opinions.
Graph Bias	Knowledge graphs may reinforce incorrect relationships between entities.	A biased knowledge graph may misrepresent historical events.

Example: Detecting Bias in Graph Embeddings

```python
python

import numpy as np
from sklearn.decomposition import PCA
import matplotlib.pyplot as plt

# Sample biased embeddings
male_vector = np.array([0.8, 0.2, 0.6])
female_vector = np.array([0.2, 0.8, 0.4])

# Apply PCA for visualization
pca = PCA(n_components=2)
embeddings = np.array([male_vector, female_vector])
reduced_embeddings = pca.fit_transform(embeddings)

# Plot bias in embeddings
plt.scatter(reduced_embeddings[:, 0], reduced_embeddings[:,
1], c=['blue', 'pink'])
plt.text(reduced_embeddings[0, 0], reduced_embeddings[0, 1],
'Male', fontsize=12)
plt.text(reduced_embeddings[1, 0], reduced_embeddings[1, 1],
'Female', fontsize=12)
plt.xlabel("PCA Component 1")
plt.ylabel("PCA Component 2")
plt.title("Bias in Graph Embeddings")
plt.show()
```

Solution Strategies:

- Use **diverse and representative training data**.
- Implement **bias detection and mitigation tools**.
- Introduce **fairness constraints in knowledge retrieval**.

13.1.2 Transparency and Explainability

Users must understand **why an AI system makes certain decisions**. This is particularly important in **Graph-Based RAG**, where **retrieval sources must be interpretable**.

Techniques to Improve Transparency

Technique	Description	Example
Explainable AI (XAI)	AI models provide justifications for their outputs.	An AI legal assistant explains how it retrieves case laws.
Traceability in Graph Retrieval	Users can track which nodes and edges contributed to a response.	A medical chatbot cites specific clinical studies.
Human-in-the-Loop AI	AI decisions are validated by human experts.	A financial AI tool requires analyst review for major transactions.

Example: Tracing the Retrieval Path in a Knowledge Graph

```python
def trace_retrieval(tx, query):
    """Finds the path followed by a query in the knowledge
graph."""
    result = tx.run(f"MATCH path = (n)-[*]->(m) WHERE
n.name='{query}' RETURN path")
    return [record["path"] for record in result]

# Example query
with driver.session() as session:
    path = session.read_transaction(trace_retrieval, "Machine
Learning")
    print("Retrieval Path:", path)
```

13.2 Data Privacy and Security

Graph-Based RAG systems handle **sensitive data** that requires **strong privacy and security measures**.

13.2.1 Best Practices for Data Protection

Key Strategies for Secure AI Systems:

1. **Anonymization**: Remove personally identifiable information (PII) from datasets.
2. **Differential Privacy**: Add controlled noise to queries to prevent data leakage.

3. **Access Control**: Restrict knowledge graph access based on user permissions.
4. **Secure Data Storage**: Encrypt graph databases and restrict unauthorized access.

Example: Implementing Data Encryption in Neo4j

```python
python

from neo4j import GraphDatabase

def encrypt_data(tx, node_name, encryption_key):
    """Encrypts a node's data for secure storage."""
    tx.run(f"MATCH (n {{name:'{node_name}'}}) SET
n.encrypted_data = aes_encrypt(n.data, '{encryption_key}')")

# Example usage
with driver.session() as session:
    session.write_transaction(encrypt_data, "PatientRecord",
"secureKey123")
```

13.2.2 Regulatory Compliance (GDPR, CCPA, etc.)

AI systems must **adhere to global data regulations**:

Regulation	Region	Key Requirements
GDPR	Europe	Data must be encrypted, and users have the right to request data deletion.
CCPA	California, USA	Users must be informed about data collection and usage.
HIPAA	USA (Healthcare)	Protects patient health information in AI systems.

Checklist for AI Compliance

✓ **Implement user consent mechanisms** before data collection.
✓ **Allow users to request data deletion** ("Right to be forgotten").
✓ **Log all data access events** for security audits.

13.3 Societal Impact and Future Research Directions

13.3.1 The Future of AI and Graph Technologies

Graph-Based RAG is expected to **redefine how AI systems retrieve and generate knowledge**.

Emerging Trends

Trend	Description
Multimodal Knowledge Graphs	Combining text, images, and videos for richer AI retrieval.
Graph-Enhanced Reinforcement Learning	AI agents learning dynamically from structured knowledge.
AI for Scientific Discovery	Automating research synthesis across disciplines.

Example: Multimodal Graph Retrieval

```python
G.add_edges_from([
    ("Research Paper", "PDF File"),
    ("Lecture", "YouTube Video"),
    ("Medical Condition", "X-ray Image"),
])
```

13.3.2 Balancing Innovation and Responsibility

AI development should prioritize **ethical responsibility** while fostering **technological advancement**.

Guiding Principles for Responsible AI

Principle	Implementation
Transparency	AI decisions must be explainable.

Principle	Implementation
Accountability	Developers should be responsible for model outputs.
Inclusivity	Ensure diverse representation in training data.
Security	Implement strong access controls.

Ethical Challenges and Solutions

Challenge	Solution
Hallucinated AI Responses	Implement confidence scoring for AI-generated outputs.
Data Privacy Risks	Use **federated learning** to prevent centralized data storage.
Bias in AI Decision-Making	Regularly audit AI models for fairness.

Summary

In this chapter, we covered:

- **Ethical considerations** such as **bias, fairness, and transparency** in Graph-Based RAG.
- **Data privacy best practices** and **compliance with regulations** like GDPR and CCPA.
- **Future research trends**, including **multimodal AI and graph-based reinforcement learning**.

Next Steps

The final chapter will **summarize key insights, provide implementation roadmaps, and guide readers on extending Graph-Based RAG for advanced applications**.

Chapter 14: Emerging Trends and Future Directions

As **Graph-Based Retrieval-Augmented Generation (RAG) systems** evolve, new advancements in **Large Language Models (LLMs), Graph Neural Networks (GNNs), and multimodal AI** are shaping the future of intelligent information retrieval. This chapter explores **next-generation AI architectures, multimodal integration, and key research challenges** to provide a comprehensive roadmap for the future of Graph-Based RAG.

14.1 Next-Generation LLMs and Graph Technologies

Graph-Based RAG is set to benefit from **improved LLM architectures and advancements in graph processing**. Innovations in both fields will enhance **knowledge retrieval, reasoning, and efficiency**.

14.1.1 Innovations in Model Architectures

Next-generation **LLMs** are improving **efficiency, contextual understanding, and interpretability**. Key trends include:

Innovation	Description	Expected Impact
Sparse Attention Mechanisms	Reduces computation by focusing only on relevant tokens.	Improves processing speed in long text retrieval.
Mixture of Experts (MoE)	Uses multiple specialized models instead of one monolithic model.	Reduces training costs while improving accuracy.
Memory-Augmented Transformers	LLMs with external memory to store knowledge from past queries.	Enhances long-term contextual understanding.

Example: Using a Memory-Augmented Transformer for RAG

python

```python
from transformers import AutoModel, AutoTokenizer

# Load a Transformer with memory support
tokenizer = AutoTokenizer.from_pretrained("facebook/bart-
large")
model = AutoModel.from_pretrained("facebook/bart-large")

query = "How is AI used in finance?"
memory = ["AI is used in risk management", "Financial
forecasting relies on AI models"]

# Augment input with memory
input_text = query + " Context: " + " ".join(memory)
inputs = tokenizer(input_text, return_tensors="pt")

# Generate response
output = model(**inputs)
print("Generated Response:", output)
```

14.1.2 Advances in Graph Neural Networks

Graph Neural Networks (GNNs) continue to evolve to **support larger, more complex knowledge graphs**.

Key Advancements in GNNs

Advancement	Description	Impact on Graph-Based RAG
Graph Transformers	Combines GNNs with transformers to capture global dependencies.	Improves reasoning over large graphs.
Heterogeneous Graph Learning	Learns from different node types (e.g., documents, videos, citations).	Enables multimodal knowledge retrieval.
Self-Supervised Graph Learning	Trains on unlabeled graph data without supervision	Reduces dependency on labeled datasets.

Example: Implementing a Graph Transformer for RAG

python

```python
from torch_geometric.nn import TransformerConv
```

```
import torch
import torch.nn.functional as F

# Define a Graph Transformer Model
class GraphTransformer(torch.nn.Module):
    def __init__(self, in_channels, out_channels):
        super(GraphTransformer, self).__init__()
        self.conv1 = TransformerConv(in_channels,
out_channels)
        self.conv2 = TransformerConv(out_channels,
out_channels)

    def forward(self, x, edge_index):
        x = self.conv1(x, edge_index)
        x = F.relu(x)
        x = self.conv2(x, edge_index)
        return x

# Initialize model
model = GraphTransformer(in_channels=16, out_channels=32)
print(model)
```

14.2 Integrating Multimodal Data

Future AI systems will **combine text, images, audio, and video** to improve retrieval.

14.2.1 Beyond Text and Graphs: Images, Audio, and Video

Graph-Based RAG is evolving to support **multimodal inputs**, allowing AI to process **diverse data types**.

Examples of Multimodal Graph Applications

Modality	Use Case
Text + Image	AI-driven **museum guides** that link text with historical images.
Graph + Video	AI-generated **film recommendations** based on graph similarity.
Graph + Audio	AI-powered **music retrieval systems** that connect lyrics to song graphs.

Example: Storing Multimodal Knowledge in a Graph

```python
G.add_edges_from([
    ("Research Paper", "PDF File"),
    ("Lecture", "YouTube Video"),
    ("Medical Condition", "X-ray Image"),
])
```

14.2.2 Unified Architectures for Multimodal Retrieval

A **unified RAG system** can handle **text, images, videos, and structured knowledge graphs**.

Model Type	Strength	Best Used For
CLIP (Contrastive Learning for Image-Text)	Maps images and text to the same vector space.	Searching images based on text descriptions.
Graph-Aided Multimodal Transformers	Uses graphs to organize cross-modal knowledge.	AI-powered document retrieval.
Multimodal Autoencoders	Learns from structured and unstructured data simultaneously.	Combining financial reports with stock prices.

Example: Using CLIP for Image-Based Graph Retrieval

```python
from transformers import CLIPProcessor, CLIPModel

# Load CLIP model
model = CLIPModel.from_pretrained("openai/clip-vit-base-patch32")
processor = CLIPProcessor.from_pretrained("openai/clip-vit-base-patch32")

# Define text and image inputs
text_inputs = processor(text=["Graph-based AI"], images=None,
return_tensors="pt")

# Compute similarity
outputs = model(**text_inputs)
print("Multimodal Embeddings:", outputs)
```

14.3 The Road Ahead for Graph-Based RAG

14.3.1 Research Challenges and Opportunities

Despite progress, Graph-Based RAG still faces **open research challenges**.

Key Research Challenges

Challenge	Potential Solutions
Scalability	Efficient indexing (e.g., FAISS) and distributed graph storage.
Explainability	Develop better interpretability techniques for AI-generated knowledge.
Data Bias	Implement fairness-aware training techniques.

Future Opportunities

Opportunity	Impact
Graph-Enhanced Reinforcement Learning	AI agents can learn from knowledge graphs dynamically.
AI for Interdisciplinary Research	Graph-Based RAG can connect knowledge across domains (e.g., medicine + physics).

14.3.2 Community and Collaborative Efforts

The **future of Graph-Based RAG** depends on **collaboration between researchers, open-source projects, and industry adoption**.

Key Open-Source Initiatives

Project	Description
Neo4j & ArangoDB	Open-source graph databases.
PyG (PyTorch Geometric)	Framework for deep learning on graphs.
FAISS & Annoy	Open-source libraries for vector search.

How to Contribute to AI Research

1. **Join OpenAI & Hugging Face Communities** for NLP model advancements.
2. **Collaborate on GitHub projects** related to graph retrieval.
3. **Publish research papers** on Graph-Based RAG improvements.

Summary

This chapter explored:

- **Advancements in LLMs and GNNs** for **next-gen retrieval systems**.
- **Multimodal RAG architectures** that integrate **text, images, video, and graphs**.
- **Future research directions** for **scalability, transparency, and bias mitigation**.

Appendices

This section provides additional resources for **deepening your understanding** of **Graph-Based Retrieval-Augmented Generation (RAG)**. It includes **key terminology, complete code listings, setup guides, and references to further reading materials**.

Appendix A: Glossary of Terms

This glossary defines key concepts related to **LLMs, knowledge graphs, GNNs, and RAG systems**.

A.1 Key Concepts and Definitions

Term	Definition
Large Language Model (LLM)	A deep learning model trained on vast amounts of text data to understand and generate human-like responses.
Retrieval-Augmented Generation (RAG)	A method where LLMs retrieve external knowledge before generating responses, enhancing accuracy.
Knowledge Graph	A structured database that stores relationships between entities in a graph format.
Graph Neural Network (GNN)	A deep learning model that operates on graph-structured data to learn node and edge representations.
Embedding	A vector representation of words, sentences, or graph nodes used for machine learning tasks.
Dense Retrieval	A retrieval method that uses deep learning embeddings to find semantically similar content.
Sparse Retrieval	A retrieval method based on keyword matching techniques such as TF-IDF or BM25.

Term	Definition
FAISS (Facebook AI Similarity Search)	A library for fast nearest neighbor search in high-dimensional spaces, used in RAG pipelines.
Neo4j	A popular graph database that allows querying and storing knowledge graphs.
Explainability (XAI)	Techniques that make AI models interpretable and transparent to users.
Multimodal AI	AI systems that integrate different data types such as text, images, audio, and video.
Hyperparameter Tuning	The process of optimizing machine learning model parameters to improve performance.

Appendix B: Code and Tooling Resources

This section provides **detailed code listings**, **setup scripts**, and **configuration files** for implementing **Graph-Based RAG systems**.

B.1: Full Code Listings

1. Setting Up a Knowledge Graph in Neo4j

```python
from neo4j import GraphDatabase

# Connect to Neo4j
uri = "bolt://localhost:7687"
driver = GraphDatabase.driver(uri, auth=("neo4j",
"password"))

def create_graph(tx):
    """Creates a knowledge graph with sample entities."""
    tx.run("CREATE (:Concept {name:'Artificial
Intelligence'})")
    tx.run("CREATE (:Concept {name:'Machine Learning'})")
    tx.run("MATCH (a:Concept), (b:Concept) WHERE
a.name='Machine Learning' AND b.name='Artificial
Intelligence' CREATE (a)-[:SUBSET_OF]->(b)")

# Execute transaction
with driver.session() as session:
```

```
        session.write_transaction(create_graph)
```

2. Implementing a Graph Neural Network (GNN)

python

```python
import torch
import torch.nn.functional as F
from torch_geometric.nn import GCNConv

# Define a simple GNN model
class GNN(torch.nn.Module):
    def __init__(self, in_channels, out_channels):
        super(GNN, self).__init__()
        self.conv1 = GCNConv(in_channels, 16)
        self.conv2 = GCNConv(16, out_channels)

    def forward(self, x, edge_index):
        x = self.conv1(x, edge_index)
        x = F.relu(x)
        x = self.conv2(x, edge_index)
        return x

# Example input data
edge_index = torch.tensor([[0, 1, 1, 2], [1, 0, 2, 1]],
dtype=torch.long)
x = torch.rand((3, 8))  # Node features

# Initialize and apply GNN
gnn = GNN(in_channels=8, out_channels=16)
node_embeddings = gnn(x, edge_index)

print("Node Embeddings:", node_embeddings)
```

3. Fast Nearest Neighbor Search with FAISS

python

```python
import faiss
import numpy as np

# Create FAISS index
dimension = 128  # Size of embeddings
index = faiss.IndexFlatL2(dimension)

# Generate example node embeddings
```

```
node_embeddings = np.random.rand(1000,
dimension).astype('float32')

# Add embeddings to FAISS index
index.add(node_embeddings)

# Query a similar node
query_embedding = np.random.rand(1,
dimension).astype('float32')
D, I = index.search(query_embedding, k=5)  # Retrieve top 5
similar nodes

print("Top 5 closest nodes:", I)
```

B.2: Environment Setup Scripts

1. Installing Required Libraries

sh

```
pip install torch torchvision torchaudio
pip install torch-geometric
pip install networkx
pip install neo4j
pip install faiss-cpu
pip install transformers
pip install spacy
pip install jupyterlab
pip install fastapi uvicorn
```

---

2. Dockerfile for Deploying Graph-Based RAG API

Dockerfile

```
FROM python:3.8

WORKDIR /app
COPY . /app

RUN pip install fastapi uvicorn torch faiss-cpu neo4j
transformers

CMD ["uvicorn", "api:app", "--host", "0.0.0.0", "--port",
"8000"]
```
sh

```
# Build and Run the Docker Container
```

```
docker build -t graph_rag .
docker run -p 8000:8000 graph_rag
```

Appendix C: Further Reading and References

This section provides **books, research papers, and online resources** to further explore **LLMs, Graph Neural Networks, and RAG systems**.

C.1 Recommended Books

Book Title	Author(s)	Description
Graph-Powered Machine Learning	Alessandro Negro	Covers advanced graph-based AI techniques.
Hands-On Machine Learning with Scikit-Learn, Keras, and TensorFlow	Aurélien Géron	Comprehensive guide to deep learning.
Deep Learning for Graphs	Lingfei Wu	Covers latest techniques in GNNs and graph-based AI.
Natural Language Processing with Transformers	Lewis Tunstall, Leandro von Werra, Thomas Wolf	Explains LLM architectures and fine-tuning techniques.

C.2 Research Papers

Title	Authors	Link
BERT: Pre-training of Deep Bidirectional Transformers for Language Understanding	Devlin et al.	Link
Graph Neural Networks: A Review of Methods and Applications	Wu et al.	Link
Dense Passage Retrieval for Open-Domain Question Answering	Karpukhin et al.	Link
Retrieval-Augmented Generation for Knowledge-Intensive NLP Tasks	Lewis et al.	Link

C.3 Online Resources

Resource	Type	Link
Hugging Face Transformers Documentation	Library Docs	huggingface.co/docs
Neo4j Knowledge Graph Tutorials	Course	neo4j.com/graphacademy
PyTorch Geometric (PyG) Tutorials	Library Docs	pytorch-geometric.readthedocs.io
FAISS for Efficient Vector Search	Library Docs	faiss.ai

Final Thoughts

This book has provided **a comprehensive guide** to **Graph-Based Retrieval-Augmented Generation (RAG)**, from **fundamentals to real-world applications**. As **AI continues to evolve**, Graph-Based RAG will play a **critical role in the future of information retrieval, knowledge representation, and multimodal AI**.

We encourage readers to **experiment, contribute to open-source projects, and engage with AI research communities** to advance this exciting field.

Appendix D: Troubleshooting and FAQs

Graph-Based RAG systems involve multiple **technologies, frameworks, and deployment environments**, which can lead to **unexpected issues**. This section provides solutions to **common problems**, along with **community resources for additional support**.

D.1 Common Issues and Their Solutions

1. Installation and Dependency Issues

Problem	Possible Cause	Solution
`ModuleNotFoundError: No module named 'torch'`	PyTorch is not installed or virtual environment is not activated.	Run `pip install torch torchvision torchaudio` and check the virtual environment.
GNN model does not run on GPU	CUDA is not installed, or PyTorch is not detecting GPU.	Run `torch.cuda.is_available();` if `False`, reinstall PyTorch with GPU support.
Neo4j connection issues	Neo4j database is not running, or credentials are incorrect.	Ensure Neo4j is running with `neo4j start` and verify credentials.

2. Graph Database Errors

Problem	Possible Cause	Solution
Query returns no results	Incorrect Cypher syntax or missing data.	Run `MATCH (n) RETURN n LIMIT 10` to inspect existing data.
Graph too slow to query	Too many nodes without indexing.	Use `CREATE INDEX FOR (n:Concept) ON (n.name)` to speed up queries.

3. Retrieval and Model Performance Issues

Problem	Possible Cause	Solution
LLM returns incorrect or irrelevant results	Poor retrieval quality or embedding mismatch.	Improve retrieval by tuning FAISS search parameters (`nlist`, `nprobe`).

Problem	Possible Cause	Solution
GNN outputs meaningless embeddings	Overfitting or incorrect architecture.	Increase training data and test different activation functions (e.g., ReLU, LeakyReLU).
FAISS retrieval is slow	Large dataset without clustering.	Use **IVFFlat** instead of **IndexFlatL2** for faster search.

D.2 Community Forums and Support Channels

For **ongoing support**, consider joining **developer forums and AI research communities**:

Platform	Description	Link
Hugging Face Forums	Discuss LLM fine-tuning, RAG models, and transformers.	huggingface.co/forums
Neo4j Community	Graph database queries, Cypher optimization.	community.neo4j.com
PyTorch Geometric (PyG) Discussions	GNN troubleshooting and model tuning.	github.com/pyg-team/pytorch_geometric/discussions
Stack Overflow	General AI and coding issues.	stackoverflow.com
Reddit - Machine Learning & NLP	Research discussions and troubleshooting.	reddit.com/r/MachineLearning

Appendix E: Bonus Projects and Exercises

This section contains **hands-on projects and exercises** to deepen your understanding of **Graph-Based RAG**.

E.1 Additional Hands-On Projects

Project 1: Legal Document Retrieval System

Objective: Build a **legal AI assistant** using **Graph-Based RAG** that retrieves **court cases, laws, and regulations**.

Steps:

1. **Collect legal text data** from sources like courtlistener.com.
2. **Build a legal knowledge graph** linking laws to relevant cases.
3. **Train a GNN model** to retrieve similar legal documents.
4. **Integrate FAISS** for fast text-based retrieval.
5. **Use an LLM** (e.g., GPT-4) to summarize legal texts.

Code Example: Querying Related Court Cases from Neo4j

```python
python

def get_related_cases(tx, case_name):
    """Fetches court cases related to a given case name."""
    result = tx.run(f"MATCH (c:Case)-[:CITED_BY]-
>(related:Case) WHERE c.name='{case_name}' RETURN
related.name")
    return [record["related.name"] for record in result]

# Example usage
with driver.session() as session:
    cases = session.read_transaction(get_related_cases,
"Brown v. Board of Education")
    print("Related Cases:", cases)
```

Project 2: AI-Powered Research Assistant

Objective: Create an **AI research assistant** that retrieves and summarizes **academic papers**.

Steps:

1. **Scrape metadata from ArXiv or Semantic Scholar.**
2. **Create a citation knowledge graph** linking research papers.

3. **Train a GNN model** to predict related research topics.
4. **Implement a RAG pipeline** to **retrieve relevant papers** before summarization.

Example: Fetching Papers by Topic Using a Knowledge Graph

```python
def query_papers_by_topic(tx, topic):
    """Finds academic papers related to a specific topic."""
    result = tx.run(f"MATCH (p:Paper)-[:RELATED_TO]->(:Topic
{{name:'{topic}'}}) RETURN p.name")
    return [record["p.name"] for record in result]

with driver.session() as session:
    results = session.read_transaction(query_papers_by_topic,
"Deep Learning")
    print("Related Research Papers:", results)
```

E.2 Exercises for Skill Reinforcement

Exercise 1: Improve Knowledge Graph Retrieval

- **Modify the FAISS retrieval system** to improve **accuracy**.
- **Experiment with hierarchical graph structures** to refine search results.

Exercise 2: Optimize a GNN Model for Large-Scale Graphs

- Implement **graph sampling techniques** (e.g., GraphSAGE, FastGCN).
- Train a **heterogeneous GNN** with **different node types (e.g., authors, papers, topics).**

Exercise 3: Deploy a Graph-Based RAG System as an API

- Use **FastAPI** to serve a **Graph-Based RAG model**.
- Dockerize the system and **deploy on AWS/GCP**.

Index

This index provides a quick reference to key concepts, topics, and technical implementations covered in this book on **Graph-Based Retrieval-Augmented Generation (RAG)**.

A

B

C

D

E

F

G

H

I

J

K

U

V

W

X

This **index serves as a quick reference guide** for **navigating key concepts, implementations, and advanced topics in Graph-Based RAG.**

www.ingramcontent.com/pod-product-compliance
Lightning Source LLC
LaVergne TN
LVHW081530050326
832903LV00025B/1715